— Advance Praise for *Hope in the Color Purple*

The Reverend Dr. Jean Kim is a proven advocate and champion of the homeless. Her autobiography offers clear insights into the soul behind the service. Her experience is instructive and at times sorrowful. Hers is also a story full of hope and vision. My belief is you, too, will be drawn in by her artful storytelling and agree that if not for war and division, she was destined to follow in her maternal grandfather's footsteps by becoming a North Korean noble scholar and teacher herself (p.28). That potential storyline was abruptly altered when "even though we owned vast land and orchards, we left North Korea with empty hands, with no cash in our pockets" (p.37). The grace and mercy of God ever central in her life, her formative years were also influenced by the genuine threat of execution and exile. A difficult history to discuss, through photographs and her honest and open sharing, we are given access to a firsthand account of life in 1940s-1950s Korea. Equally as important, we are exposed to a consistent message embodied within her life and advocacy that we all should be inspired by: "I refused to be treated as an inferior, second-class human being…" (p.69). Edmonds Community College is honored to be a partner with the Jean Kim Foundation. Humbled to call her, my friend.

Dr. Steve Woodard
Dean for Student Success, Edmonds Community College
Unitarian Universalist

. . . .

Bravery, compassion, grace, love and eternal optimism. Jean Kim tells her life story spanning from North Korea to Lynnwood, Washington talking her walk through a difficult childhood to her current place of honored elder in our precious community. *Hope in the Color Purple* closes its final chapters with Jean Kim's tremendous success in providing pallet houses for students attending Edmonds Community College. Her drive to knock down barriers to human success and understanding of how to wrap around support for those who find themselves struggling to find hope in their daily life is unwavering. Many have been blessed, including me, to have crossed paths and warmed in the compassionate glow of dear Jean Kim. It was a painful delight to journey in the shoes of Jean through her *Hope in the Color Purple* memoir.

Mayor Nicola Smith
Lynnwood, WA

As one of the purple people that Rev. Jean Kim loved and served, it is amazing to be able to read what put the fire in her soul to help homeless people. From all my interactions with the Rev. Jean I would have never guessed that she would have gone through such hardships like she did. Her story is truly inspiring me to want to use my hardships of being homeless toward something that can help others going through similar hardships. I hope one day I can gain the strength that is inside Rev. Jean to continue to fight while still going through so many struggles.

Robert Okerstrom
Homeless Student at Edmonds Community College

. . . .

Dr. Reverend Jean Kim is the living definition of what the love and compassion of Jesus Christ demonstrated. Her story and vision she depicts in this book gave me a whole different perspective on life and the "American Dream." I first met Jean Kim when I was broken, beaten, and homeless with five children and pregnant. Caught in the cycles of poverty, mental illness, and addictions as she so accurately describes in her story, is also my story. On page 13 Jean states, "I truly hope that all "pain-stricken purple people" in this world can be transformed into "hope-filled purple people". I am writing here to validate the authenticity of this statement. Thank you, Reverend Jean Kim, for being a light in my cold, dark world and giving me the hope and support that I will continue on to give others. Thank you for the honor of reading your story. You are my mentor and fellow sister in Christ. May "His" work continues on.

Michelle Grunder
Edmonds Community College Graduate/Student
Social/Human Services Professional Advocate
"Hope-filled purple person"

. . . .

I am the oldest of Rev. Jean Kim's grandchildren. I am studying dentistry at the University of Washington, and my grandma is so proud of me. My grandma pours out her life and soul into telling a story of purple in a way that enlightens us of grueling hardships that she endured. She wrote this autobiography for us (John, Nina, and I) to not wonder where we came from, and we are forever grateful for the gift of sharing her story with us. Though written for us, I am convinced that her story is a brilliant example for all to see how perseverance, compassion, and purpose can come together in one tiny human being and make a difference in the world today.

Paul Kim, Grandson

HOPE
IN THE COLOR
PURPLE

A Life and Mission of a Thousand Pains and Ten Thousand Troubles

TO _Donald Gary_

*Abundant blessings on you and
your family with good health,
peace, hopes, dreams and
all the success.*

Author: _[signature]_

Jean Kim _1/19/19_

"God carries me on her back."

When I was seven or eight years old, I was often sick with malaria and suffered from fever and chills. My mother would carry me on her back and the feeling of comfort would make me sleep for several hours. Her back was my warm bed, my comfort and my refuge.

Later in life reflecting upon my life's achievement it was not I who had done any of it, but it was God who carried me on her back and ran or flew to take me to the right place at the right time to do the right thing because "I am slow, incompetent, and incomplete with chronic illness." It was from this experience that I often exclaimed that God has carried me on her back when my heart aches in heavy grief or despair. I attribute all my accomplishments to the grace and mercy of God. God has been carrying me on her back and placed me where I am today. Even today as I serve homeless students I am using the same expression "God carries me on her back."

HOPE
IN THE COLOR
PURPLE

A Life and Mission of a Thousand Pains and Ten Thousand Troubles

by
Reverend Jean Kim

HOPE *in the Color* PURPLE

A Life and Mission of a Thousand Pains and Ten Thousand Troubles

For inquiries or for those who cannot
order online, please contact:
Nina Kim (425) 789-6843

If you would like to make a contribution toward
the assistance of people who struggle to end their
poverty and/or homelessness, please send a check
payable to the **Hope in the Color Purple Fund**
and mail it to: c/o Nina Kim
15228 72nd Dr. SE, Snohomish, WA 98296

Book cover and interior design by
Lanphear Design
www.lanpheardesign.com

Cover Illustration: Stephanie Shinn

Library of Congress Cataloging-in-Publication Data
Hope in the Color Purple/
Reverend Jean Kim.

ISBN: 9781790589098

Contents

Foreword

Meeting Rev. Jean Kim, Seattle's "Mother of the Homeless" was by accident, as most of my important encounters have been. Rev. Kim, whom I met in Torrance, California, in 2015, was really a "woman of the color purple." Her neatly groomed white hair and graceful expression impressed me, but the shirt she was wearing that matched all of her possessions was especially distinctive. In her appearance I detected a hint of an uncommon spirit. It was the warmth of her large heart, which she earned like a medal through a thousand bitter afflictions, trials, tribulations, and soul-piercing pain that led her to embrace and serve her homeless friends. There couldn't have been any better balm than her entirely giving warm love that heals homeless friends who suffer from physical, emotional, and spiritual poverty, and disease unto death, in such an affluent world.

While I was reading her painful life story I was sucked into her purple life and mission as if I had received an electric shock. I was overcome with inspiration, pity, and pain. Her story carried me deep into the night till the break of dawn. It kept me awake through the entire night and continued into the next day. I was deeply inspired by the mystery of one person's life and the wonder of God's work through her. It was a striking revelation for me.

My accidental encounter with her thus led me to play a midwife's role in giving birth to the story of her life and mission into this volume, *Hope in the Color Purple* (in Korean, 2017). This work was an honor and reward for me because it was a rarely given blessing for me to publish such a precious story; not everyone will experience such a blessing. I feel excited imagining readers sharing the same feelings of inspiration, shock, and blessing as I experienced that night while reading this book.

The story begins with her birth in Ham Heung City in North Korea in the era of Japanese occupation, then escaping at age eleven, on foot, holding her brother's hand. There are many days and nights fleeing a communist regime to South Korea, and pain and suffering during the Korean War and exile. There is her battle with poverty, and her struggle to overcome the old customs of male dominance over women. She takes on the latter during her academic journey, including graduating from Ewah

Girls' High School and entering Han Shin Theological Seminary. Later she goes abroad to the U.S. for advanced study, where she experiences the change of life caused by the death of her oldest son, and participates in the democratic movement for South Korea—all of which became the foundation that pulled her into her homeless mission and giving her entire life in obedience … all of these stories were more traumatic and deeply inspirational than any movie or novel could ever be.

Seeing one person's unending effort to burn up her last ounce of energy by sparking the last flame for the homeless is like seeing and feeling the image of incarnated God's love and grace.

As purple signifies the meaning of the Lent season in Christian tradition during the forty days prior to Easter, every day she lives Lent in her purple shirts for and with the homeless people.

In her book, Rev. Kim awakens us to the paradoxical reality that every city has homeless people in the country called the United States where "affluent" is known to be a pronoun. And then she attempts to answer the question of why faith communities and churches must be engaged in the homeless mission and how to do it by taking us through the biblical understanding of poverty and homelessness and by sharing the experience she gained throughout her own life.

For over fifty years her focus has been on ending homelessness. She cares for the homeless in loving heart, teaches, empowers, uplifts, and cries with them, and at times wanders around with them looking for solutions. Such an unending and unchanging effort for and with them made her the mother, sister, and friend of the homeless people. When they call her Jean the word carries a feeling and nuance of mother, sister, and friend of the homeless people themselves who all feel so close to her. Therefore, she is their family and their home.

She celebrated her sixtieth as well as eightieth birthday with them and for them. She hopes to give them the final gift that she will get the day when she will be laid out. I pray that such a life will contribute to the future direction of and be the content of the homeless mission.

I thank and honor God for allowing me to publish Rev. Kim's memorial-like autobiography in Korean.

Esther Park, Publisher, iwithjesus
Seoul, Korea 2016

Preface

As I grew old I felt frustrated that I didn't know much about my parents' families, especially about my maternal grandfather! Had I known more about my family, I would have known more clearly where I came from.

When I was young I was often undeservedly called "bright," "intelligent," and "genius" by my family members, relatives, and even seminary professors. I began wondering where my brightness came from, if I had it. All I heard from my mother was that my grandfather was a noble scholar and held an office in the ancient Korean government. So if I had academic talents, I must have inherited DNA from my maternal side of the family.

So much frustration over not knowing my roots clearly motivated me to leave something in writing for my grandchildren, lest they go through the same frustration as I had. So I started to write something down in English for my grandchildren (whose language is English). I had no intention of publishing it, because I am not a good writer and was scared to expose all of my painful memories to the world.

But then, once a Korean clergy woman Soon Hee Earm happened to be in Seattle attending the same conference that I was attending and happened to stay at my home with a few other friends. After all others left, she kept staying with me for another week due to a change of her plane schedule. She urged me to write my story in Korean to encourage Korean women living a pain-stricken life. For the whole week, she willingly cooked for me so that I could focus on writing. Believe it or not, within a week, half of my story was written. After she left, within a month, a draft of my story was done. I was amazed how my stories were stored neatly in my brain in a chronological order. Writing them was no problem although they brought back all my painful memories and made me weep a lot. I stored the draft (in Korean) in my computer.

Then I happened to run into Esther Park, a total stranger, in L.A. at our common friend's home, where she and I happened to stay one night. Our common friend, Suhn Park urged us to meet and talk—one was a publisher and the other was a storyteller. We were busy with other commitments, but talked till bedtime and continued the next day while we were walking in a park. She wanted to take my story to Korea.

She was a brave woman who published the book knowing that I didn't have a penny to pay for the cost. Her writing in the above preface about my story is beyond overwhelming.

This book seems to begin with God's doing and end with God's doing! It is my story, but it is also God's story and the story of purple (homeless) people.

Miraculously, relatives and friends contributed so generously that, to everyone's surprise, the publisher's cost has been covered. This is another miracle story of **God's doing.**

Now, English-speaking friends in Seattle and other areas including my grandchildren urged me to finish my English version. That's exactly what I started to do. It was only a matter of finishing and polishing since I had it halfway done before.

My Korean publisher had done a wonderful job in weaving my story with homelessness stories. That's the format I am going to follow here because my story is their story and vice versa.

I also tried to revise a little by adding more examples of homeless missions for those who want to look at them and glean some information.

Purple is My Color

I am called the "purple pastor" by many of my friends. I earned the title from people who have seen me in a purple shirt every day since 1997 with the words "End Homelessness" printed on it. Therefore, the purple color happened to become my identity.

Purple is the liturgical color for the Season of Lent in Christian tradition. It can symbolize pain, suffering, mourning and penitence. It is also the color of royalty, so traditionally it has also been used for the season of Advent in Christian tradition.

Lent is the time Christians grieve and lament for Jesus's suffering, reflect upon our lives seriously in prayer and fasting, repent our personal and corporate sins and commit to serve the Lord more faithfully. Likewise, in my purple shirt, I grieve, lament, and repent for having so many homeless people in this affluent country, and commit to love and serve Jesus Christ by serving the homeless and working toward ending homelessness.

For this reason, I chose purple when I developed shirts with a message, "End Homelessness for all People" as a campaign of the National Presbyterian Church (U.S.A.). Therefore, purple became not only my personal identity but also my homeless mission color.

Because purple can also symbolize the pain, suffering, and mourning of homeless people who lost everything, including their jobs, homes, families, identity, health, pride, joy and dreams, they deserve to be called "Purple People."

Purple also represents my own personal pain, suffering, and mourning for my past hurts and wounds. Therefore, Jesus, my homeless friends, and I share our pain with each other. Thus, my love for Jesus is my love for the homeless and my love for the homeless is my love for Jesus. As Jesus participates in my suffering and pain, I, too, participate in his as well as my homeless friend's. Therefore, every day is Lent for me in my purple shirt. My life is a purple life, and I am glad to be called the "Woman in Purple." So, I call the Lord "Jesus in Purple," my homeless friends "People in Purple," and my service for the poor "Mission in Purple." I enjoy living

Lent every day of my life. Here is why:

1. Lent begins with Ash Wednesday and ends with Easter Sunday. Ash Wednesday starts **40 days** prior to Easter. The concept of the number **40** comes from Jesus's fasting for **40 days**. Mentioned 146 times in scripture, the number **40** generally symbolizes a period of testing, trial, or probation.

2. Matthew 4:1-11 reports that Jesus, full of the Holy Spirit, returned from his baptism in Jordan and was led by the Spirit in the wilderness, where for **forty** days he was tempted by the devil. [2]

3. In his baptism, he confirmed his identity as **the beloved son of God**. And he was led into temptation to further confirm what kind of Messiah **this beloved son of God** must become. He was challenged by an idea of a materially wealthy or powerful and mighty Messiah as Israel was expecting a Messiah to be.

4. Had he chosen all these identities as the devil suggested he should have gone to Jerusalem Palace or temple, or the White House in Washington, DC, or Trump Tower in New York.

5. Matthew 4:12-16 reports that instead, he went to **Galilee** of the Gentiles—the people who sat in **darkness**—to launch his first mission choosing the neediest region **as his mission site**. [16]

6. Matthew 4:24 reports that those people who were sitting in **darkness** were not only poor but were sick, afflicted with various diseases and pains, demoniacs, epileptics, and paralytics.

7. Luke 4:18 further reports that his **purpose** was to bring good news to the poor; to proclaim release to the captives, recovery of sight to the blind, to let the oppressed go free, and to proclaim the year of Jubilee. [19]

8. Finally, he goes to **Jerusalem** to face his **passion for the poor** (materially, emotionally, socially, and spiritually homeless) because he loved them dearly.

9. **Jesus's humble march** in to Jerusalem on Palm Sunday is in contrast to the march of Roman soldiers showing off their power and making threats. He marched in with all the poor, afflicted, and displaced ones while the Romans' march was to impose more of such afflictions on

already broken people. While Jesus's march was **to save people**, the Romans' march was to arrest and kill anyone who opposed Roman policies.

I was deeply attracted to this image of Jesus ever since my teen years. Modeling after this Jesus, I chose to serve the neediest, poorest, and most vulnerable people. After serving them for half a century, those I chose to serve now are current and potential adult college students who are physically and/or emotionally, mentally, and legally challenged; struggle with rental, housing, economic, and employment barriers; and live in poverty and/or homelessness. Therefore, the crowd Jesus served resembles the one I serve today. This is my way of living Lent every day.

Hope in the Color Purple

As many Christians believe, Jesus's life didn't just end with suffering but brought hope to all humanity by his resurrection. His resurrection story gives all the suffering tremendous hope that people don't have to suffer forever but can overcome it and obtain everlasting hope. Therefore, **purple**, which signifies pain and suffering can also bring **hope** to all troubled people as Jesus's cross did. Since that happened to my life I am hoping the same thing can happen to many troubled and suffering people. Thus, the purple of **pain** can be transformed into a purple of **hope**. I truly hope that all "**pain-stricken purple people**" in this world can be transformed into "**hope-filled purple people**."

Gratitude

I needed lots of support and encouragement to write this volume. Huge thanks and gratitude go to Rev. Soon Hee Earm who encouraged and urged me to write my story. Colleagues of the Nest Mission and my son and daughter-in-law and grandchildren who not only walked with me throughout the journey, but also offered me financial and emotional support. Special thanks go to Steve and Marcy Hong, Rev. Mickie Choi and Chan Hie Park, who allowed me to hide out at their Rancho Cucamonga, Laguna Wood and Santa Ana homes, respectfully, while I was doing my writing work and Jasmine, the Hong's daughter, Paul Han and Rev. Shin Hwa Park, Rev. Esther Na and her sister Ha Na Na, and Cecilia Kim all in Southern California and who all supplied my needs while I was away from my Seattle home and writing. Very special gratitude goes to Steve Hong, Paul Han, and Chan Hie Park for taking care of me while I was writing but fell ill in California.

And I owe immense thanks to Esther Park, the publisher iwithjesus, who bravely committed to publish my Korean version knowing that I have no financial competence to pay for her work. I also owe a huge gratitude to Rev. Myung Ja Yue (Indiana), Richard Wu (Seattle, Washington), Clair Kim (Maryland), Rev. Kwang Soo Kim (Chicago, Illinois) and my dear son and daughter-in-law (Snohomish, Washington) for assuming the cost of publication of this English version. I also thank my grandchildren for reading the manuscript. And lastly, I thank Monica James for the wonderful editing work and Robert Lanphear for publishing this material.

When I stand before my audience, I usually start my talk by expressing my gratitude as follows:

I am standing before you as your mission product in Korea. I met Jesus at Ewah Girl's High School (1949–1955), which was founded by American Methodist missionaries. And I grew up in the Presbyterian Church, Korea.

I am standing before you as one of million lives that were saved in the Korean War by the sacrifice of American/U.N. soldiers.

I am standing before you as one who cannot take for granted the abundant blessings I have received in this country. I am profoundly grateful, and thus share my life with the purple people around me.

Therefore, I am standing before you as a voice of our homeless sisters and brothers whom I love and serve because we reside in each other, and they go with me everywhere I go. Thus, they speak through my voice and I speak from their pain-stricken hearts.

PART ONE

Search for Roots and Memories

CHAPTER 1

Seeds Planted on the Streets

The street is usually concrete, so hard and cold that any seed can hardly survive there. Did I plant any seeds there? Am I out of my mind thinking of planting seeds on the paved street? From the outset, readers can tell what an impossible mission I am talking about!

People I serve include the poor/homeless adults, seniors, veterans, racial ethnic minorities, domestic violence survivors, immigrants, and whoever wants to pursue a college education and job training. They are economically impoverished Washington state residents. Many of them are on some form of government assistance, such as food stamps, which qualifies them for federal student aid for college. Many of them live on the streets and/or in their cars. Some check in and out of motels and move around from couch to couch (couch surfing), while some live in low-income subsidized housing. Many work but earn such a meager amount that they can't afford housing.

Many suffer from various forms of mental-health challenges—depression, bipolar disorder, schizophrenia, post-traumatic stress disorder (PTSD), attention deficit hyperactivity disorder (ADHD), personality disorders, anxiety disorders, seizures, and more—along with substance abuse and legal troubles. Many seem to suffer from emotional challenges—immature development or growth due to lack of a support system when they grew up. Most of us had parents who loved and cared for us and acted as our mentors. However, many of our homeless friends were missing such parental support in their early life and didn't grow into a healthy, mature adulthood. Many of us are fortunate to maintain a social support system with our family members, relatives and friends. But many of our homeless friends in general have had little social support for most of their lives because they were reared in broken homes or by emotionally challenged parental figures or foster parents, many of whom were often involved with substance use, and abuse of their children physically, emotionally, and sexually. Therefore, many of our homeless friends' behaviors and coping skills are often challenges to themselves and society. However, they are not intellectually retarded; rather, they are bright and intelligent. All of them have God-given potential, possibility, and hope as God's children.

Living without a place to call home is stressful, especially for students. They attend classes disheveled, dirty, smelly, and very obviously homeless. Such a condition not only distracts from their schoolwork and that of their peers, but it is embarrassing, degrading, and depressing. Homeless students report chronic fatigue due to lack of sleep caused by living on the streets or in uncomfortable cars, or in the woods and being exposed to unbearable temperatures and snow or rain. Some say they must sleep outside with one eye open lest a police officer gives them a ticket or arrests them for trespassing. The constant lack of security for themselves and their possessions leaves them emotionally and mentally fatigued and extremely stressed out.

With life on the streets, pre-existing physical conditions such as high blood pressure, diabetes, obesity, heart and liver problems, substance abuse, and chronic pain from past injuries, as well as learning disabilities or many other ailments, can all become much worse. In addition to the exacerbation of preexisting conditions, they pick up new conditions and diseases as well. As a result, most homeless students are prone to accidents and/or illness.

This leaves many homeless students in general too sick to perform well in school or obtain and retain employment, but not sick enough to qualify for government assistance based on physical or emotional disabilities. These challenges cause their academic performance to suffer greatly and they become discouraged. Getting into community colleges or four-year colleges with hope, keeping up with studies, handling long-lasting emotional struggles as well as many daily obstacles proves to be a huge challenge for our students, which contributes to their dropping out of school. **These are the hard-concrete streets where I plant seeds of hope in purple people.**

Here are a few examples of how hard it is for seeds to survive on the concrete streets: I had planted a seed in a fifty-year-old man who started to attend a community college. With all my support, nurture, and watering he was able to go for a while, but his preexisting emotional issues made him quit. This seed couldn't survive on a concrete street.

Whenever someone quits my heart is broken not only because I invest a lot of time, love, energy, and effort for that one soul, but also because one little seed I planted on the streets fades away or dies.

But not all seeds I plant on the streets dry out or are eaten by birds, but some survive. After that gentleman of age fifty, eleven students challenged to enroll in Edmonds Community College. When the spring quarter was over, two dropped out. And I happened to take a trip to Korea. When I returned a month later, two had moved away, two others quit because they felt it was hard for them to survive, and two more quit for their own or family sickness. So when I returned only three were still in school. Again, streets were too tough for seeds to survive and grow, except for a strong three seeds.

Those who survived are seeds of our hopes. There is worth to our efforts. There is a future. We see more of these seeds that are growing:

One woman studying medical billing got high achievement scores and she was so happy and excited that she placed her report card right in front of my eyes with a huge proud smile. Her husband attends a Washington technical college. She suffers from an injured hip bone and worn-out cartridge. Doctors keep putting her surgery off. She can now barely walk with a cane. Finally, she couldn't get around any longer, including attending classes. Now, while she awaits her surgery date, she takes online courses at home. This couple had never stopped a single quarter to attend classes. They live on a shoestring income from student financial aid and his part-time work, and often run into lack of money to pay for rent. We helped her several times. She and her husband are very strong seeds that survive on the hard, cold concrete streets.

These people are showing God-given potential and possibilities that are God-given natural nutrients no one can take away.

Many others are trying very hard to keep up with their studies and work part-time jobs with meager earnings due to lack of education and/or job skills. Many are also unemployed due to emotional and physical challenges along with not enough jobs to go around for all who want to work.

For many people who have been out of school for so long, getting into college is a tremendous challenge. Keeping up with studies is an even bigger challenge. It is a struggle for them to go to school in their brutal homeless life. They have to fight with health and financial issues, with ordinances that show little mercy to the homeless. They carry many traffic tickets and citations for public drinking, sleeping, loitering, and smoking. They have to fight with all the stumbling blocks from their past incarceration histories and debts, with shelter/social service systems, including low-income housing systems. They have to fight for sleeping and parking spots every night, for restrooms and showers. They have to fight with bad weather, with robbery, violence, and assault in their street life.

They also must fight through their own habits of a chaotic and careless lifestyle that was developed in street life. They must fight with their forgetfulness, excuses, irresponsibility, physical or emotional challenges, addictions, and unhealthy habits. They must struggle to keep appointments, be responsible and attend classes regularly, and finish school tasks on time. They must fight for food, money, love, recognition, and pride. They must fight with despair, discouragement, and hopelessness. They must fight with temptation to use substances or drop out of school. Some homeless people are exceptionally honest, reliable, and responsible; but for many, these are challenges they must overcome. For all of these reasons, their everyday life is a struggle and a fight. Their ardent desire to enhance their education can easily be diminished by these many obstacles and barriers that we can call the "concrete road."

A Thousand Hot Peppers and Ten Thousand Hardships

To express such a painful life I adopted four Chinese words (Koreans pronounce them *chon shin man ko*, meaning "a thousand hot peppers, ten thousand hardships"). I would call it "a *thousand pains and ten thousand troubles*."

The mission of planting these seeds on the concrete road is like digging it with bare hands; it is so hard, painful, and stressful that it deserves to be called Chon Shin Man Ko "a thousand pains and ten thousand troubles."

However, despite all that, our homeless friends still have God-given goodness, great potential, and hope. But without help in meeting their needs, it is not possible for them to attain their educational goals, and they would easily drop out of the race. Therefore, to prevent drop outs and help our homeless friends achieve academic success, which will lead to a self-sufficient and significantly enhanced life, an on-going case-management service—tools, top soil, water, nutrients—with crisis intervention is absolutely required.

However, the above "Chon Shin Man Ko" is not just a story of our homeless students/friends but our own story as well. Now I am moving on to share my own "Chon Shin Man Ko" homeless story:

CHAPTER 2

Ham Heung City, My Roots

I was born in 1935 as the youngest of three siblings to wealthy parents. In Won Kim was my educated wealthy father and Hyo Sook Park was my uneducated mother, a highly noble scholar's daughter in Ham Heung City, Ham Kyung Namdo, North Korea. I was told we lived in Ham Heung City at first and then moved to Sun Duck, a countryside where my father inherited huge estates and farmlands and three huge orchards from his father.

Once upon a time, Ham Heung City was used to banish political criminals. So it is said that there are many descendants of highly educated and cultured people in that city. It is said that the winter temperature is bitter and that people in that region are strong survivors. Ham Heung was rather modernized because it accepted Western civilization early on through Christian missionaries. Ham Heung City is known especially for its modernized kitchen and its built-in dish cabinets in which beautiful dishes were stacked up and displayed showing them off through sliding glass doors. Most kitchens in other cities were very primitive with no such luxuries.

The political climate at the time of my birth was uneasy as it was during the Japanese invasion and occupation of Korea (1919–1945). We were all given a Japanese name and forced to speak Japanese. We all lost our identity and nationality. We were forced to sing the Japanese national anthem. If we sang our own, we were arrested and punished. We couldn't own or fly Korean flags. If we were found with one, we paid the price for it. Early on I learned all about oppression. I lived under such a political system for the first ten years of my life.

CHAPTER 3

Early Childhood

Material Wealth and Emotional Poverty

I remember that I was raised like a little princess materially, eating special food, wearing beautiful clothes, and living in a beautiful home. When my father came home sporadically he beat my mother.

Father's Abuse

My father, a highly educated, wealthy and capable leader in the community was a very violent person who abused my mother and two older brothers severely.

Whenever he came home he checked our report cards. He checked mine, too, but didn't comment, perhaps because mine was always good. I imagine we feared him so that we had to study hard. We had never done anything together with our father.

One night my sporadic father came home after a time away with other women and he checked my brothers' report cards. When he wasn't satisfied with their grades, he beat my mother and blamed her for not monitoring their schoolwork. He beat her and dragged her by the hair to the kitchen, all the while threatening to burn her in the oven. We would all scream in horror trying to stop him from burning our mom. It was the most cruel, cold-blooded, and hair-raising experience. Whenever I recall that incident, to this day I still feel the chill and horror, and can hardly breathe.

Although he didn't put his hands on me, it didn't help with my self-esteem as a "girl." I grew up hating being a girl. I learned to think that girls were born to be used and abused. I grew up thinking all men were abusers.

From that experience, early on I learned that **education was very important.** It could have begun as a subconsciously ingrained belief that if I did well in school, neither I nor my mother would be punished. While I had never recognized this unconscious fear, I never missed school even when I was sick. I have been a good student all my life up to my old age.

Our education was very important to our mom even without my father's punishment because she came from a highly educated family. My maternal grandfather was a noble scholar and a teacher in North Korea. In those days, you had to be very highly educated to take up an office in the government. My mother remembered when her father received pension checks from the government, which means he held a prominent position. He had to change into public official's attire, spread out a mat on the ground, sit on it, bow toward the king's palace, and graciously receive the check. My maternal grandfather didn't have another wife. He was a very

My mother Hyo Sook Park

respected scholar who taught many children in those days, including the boy who became the CEO of the Sam Pyo Soy Sauce Company in Seoul, Korea. He used to bring us a gift of soy sauce every New Year's Eve because my mother was his teacher's daughter. My mother taught herself by overhearing what the boys were memorizing out loud while she was working in the kitchen near their class. She said she used to write words on the clay kitchen floor. In those days, school was going on in the teacher's home.

She became literate this way. I remember that she used to read novels at night and wrote letters to my bothers. During this period in Korea, girls were not allowed to attend school, so my maternal grandmother was an uneducated homemaker.

I remember my mother always grieved for her lack of education. My mother's credo for me was *"you don't have to marry, know how to cook, clean, and wash but get all the education you can get, stand on your own feet and don't allow men to abuse you."* It is because of my mother's credo that I set out to be a student forever; I was 71 when I got my Doctor of Ministry degree from San Francisco Theological Seminary.

My mother was a very bright woman. She passed away in 1982 at the age of 84. She was born in 1898. She retained her good memory until her last breath. I wish I could be that way too. I carry a hardworking, faithful, honest, and proud, bright mother in my soul. She was a good role model for me as a strong, responsible woman who stood up for her own rights even during violence. My attitude about work was shaped by my mother's workaholism. I turned out to be a workaholic too.

At another time, while my mother was working on her vegetable garden, my father beat her, kicking her so hard that he broke her back. At that time, as I later heard, she determined to end her life by starving despite the neighbor's help. So I got a bowl of gruel in a tightly closed container that our neighbor lady put on my back and tied it with a towel. I brought it to my mom to eat. Looking at me, she felt compassion for me and couldn't die, leaving me behind; I was five years old then. So she began to eat the food I brought for her.

Yet another time, my father didn't want my mother to sell apples. That was the only income source to educate the children. He and my mother argued, and my father beat my mother. My second-oldest brother, Chin Woo, got so angry that he picked up the orchard gate and threw it into the rice field next to the orchard. My father got angry at him and came down and beat my mother more, destroying furniture, etc., because he couldn't find Chin Woo, who was hiding. That day Chin Woo went to my father's house and knocked father's dish cabinet onto the kitchen floor. It was a war between the son and the father. The angry father expelled us to Sun Duck village, two and a half miles away from him. Sun Duck was a small town where there were stores, a market, my school, and government offices. My father bought a house and expelled us there. Perhaps he finally realized the impossibility of keeping two families so close in the same village.

I remember from early on I thought I would never marry a man. I even regretted being born a girl, although I wasn't physically abused by him except for witnessing his abuse on my mother and brothers. Therefore, when he was not home with us, we were happy and at peace. But when he came home, we were swallowed up by chaos and fear. I don't ever recall doing anything fun or memorable with my father as a family. We didn't want anything to do with him. He had never talked to us except punishing us. Oddly, I was the only one he called out by my name and didn't physically abuse. Sometimes, even in hatred I thought he must have liked me. All of us were very angry with our father.

Drowned in My Mother's Tears

Emotionally, my childhood was filled with my mother's tears, grief and anguish: they were my daily food. Whenever she cried, I cried with her. I shared all her tears, anguish, grief, and anger. In my early life, I had inherited all her somatic illness. So I had a sickly childhood with various physical symptoms. Especially every winter, when I would have bronchitis with a severe cough for many months. My mother told me that ever since I got sick with whooping cough at age five, I got into the habit of suffering from severe bronchitis every cold season. That habit has lasted even up to this day at age 83. Now it is developing into lung fibrosis, which will eventually take my last breath.

Illness

I remember being a sickly child. In winter I was sick with bronchitis and malaria in summer and constant tummy trouble. My mother used to take me to a doctor in Ham Heung City. To get to the bus, she had to walk for an hour. She must have carried me on her back all that distance. Once I stayed at the doctor's home, which could have been a hospitalization. Later, I heard the doctor was my father's friend. So, if I incurred a doctor's bill, my father must have gone around and paid for it.

My Mother's Back, God's Back

When I was seven or eight years old, I was often sick with malaria. I suffered from fever and chills, which were typical symptoms. This usually happened in the sizzling summer months. When the fever started at school, my teacher would send me home. Usually in the morning and after school, several kids would come and go together. But in this case, I had to walk alone, over two miles to go home. On the way home, I would sit on the roadside and rest under the hot sun, which made me feel good because I was having chills. When I finally reached home, I'd nearly pass out from the fever. Then my mother would carry me, and the feeling of comfort would make me sleep for several hours on her back. When I'd waken up on her back, I'd feel better, with the fever long subsided. Whenever I was unhappy or cried, she would carry me on her back. Her back was my warm bed, and my comfort and my refuge.

A confession has born out of this experience that God carries me on her back when my heart aches in a heavy grief or despair. Reflecting upon my life's achievement it was not I who have done any of it, but it was God who carried me on her back and ran or flew to take me to a right place at the right time to do the right thing because "I am slow, incompetent, and incomplete with chronic illness." I often confess that God had been carrying me on her back when I was on a speaking tour on behalf of the Presbyterian Church (U.S.A.). Otherwise how could I have boarded the plane one hundred eighty-four times and spoken to 430 groups in 6 years. This means I boarded the plane 31 times per year and spoke to 71 churches/groups per year. My confession is that God flew me on her back to so many places at God's speed. I attribute all my accomplishments to the grace and mercy of God. God has been carrying me on her back and placed me where I am today. Even today as I serve homeless students I am using the same expression "God carries me on her back."

This time I use a feminine noun for God because I can relate my mother's warmth and comfort to God's. My father's abusive behavior ruined my masculine image of God. This means that many children who have been abused by their fathers or witness to their abuse find it hard to relate to God as the "father" God.

My Brothers

My parents' first son, I heard, died in his infancy. Until age ten, I was like a little princess with my two older brothers, while many other people in the village were farmers or fishermen and very poor.

My brothers were both sent to cities to go to school. My eldest brother, Chin Ho, was sent to Seoul to attend Bo Sung High School and then to Japan for college. Only wealthy families could do this in those days. My other brother, Chin Woo was sent to Ham Heung City to attend high school. I heard he was always in trouble at school, perhaps because he was an angry boy. So I don't know about my brothers' younger days because I wasn't there; we were fifteen and eight years apart. For so many years my mother and I lived on our own after the boys were sent to school in big cities.

My mother told me that my oldest brother, Chin Ho, tenderly loved and cared for me in my infancy when mother was away to market. He often babysat me. He would wash all the diapers and fold them as a woman would do. He was a neat, pleasant, good-looking man and most girls loved him. He checked the length of my skirt, it had to go above knees which was unusual in those days. He lifted my head with his both hands saying "see, Seoul city, where I

My oldest brother, Chin Ho Kim

am going to send you there to be educated." In those days, from North Korea going to school in Seoul, the capital city, was such an honorable thing. His love and vision for me made me who I am today. He was always a loving father figure for me. When I attended grade school he

My second oldest brother, Chin Woo Kim

used to give me lots of positive strokes, way more than my father did. My brothers used to introduce me fondly to their friends: "This is my little sister." I was bonded very closely to my brothers, especially to my oldest brother. He always uplifted the smart side of me. When we came to Seoul later, he promised to send me to be educated in the United States, which was also such a challenging thing to do that people used to say "it's like picking stars from heaven." Before he fulfilled that promise, the Korean War took his life. (He was a Korean Army Lieutenant.) I didn't realize what his positive strokes did to me until later in my life. I thank God that he was in my life.

Beautiful Hometown

In that country my family was so rich that we used to own four homes. There was a house in each orchard. In the main home, at the foothill of a mountain, my paternal grandparents must have lived. It was a well built one, better than our neighbor's clay homes. From the main home we could look down the whole village over which we could see a glimpse of a river. We had a small orchard behind our main house. I used to climb up an apple tree to get fruit that was so well ripened the birds loved to eat it. I used to get up early to pick chestnuts in the back of the orchard, at the foothill. During the night they fell on the ground. We had a little natural spring at the foothill that supplied our drinking water. Flowers were blooming all around the main house in the summer. My hometown, and especially our house, was sitting on a beautiful high spot. Had I been an artist I would have drawn a picture of it.

Our house was distant from our neighbors: There was no house behind or left side of us. There was one on the distant right side and one below my house. Both were a block away from us.

My father and his second wife lived in the main house later. For some time, my mother, two bothers, and I lived in a tiny house (let me call it No. 2 house) next to the main house sharing a huge yard and the toilet house. I don't think we lived there too long. After my father moved to the third house half a mile away, we got to live in the main house. After we moved into the main house, my mother turned the little No. 2 house, which was in between the main house and the toilet house, into storage. The storage house had several rooms. One room was for apple storage. Another was for chestnuts. (I liked dried chestnuts. One bite could tell if it was dried because the dried ones were soft. Then I would eat it. If not, I would throw it back in.) And yet another room was for crops. Another one my mother used to change her clothes when she came back from her outings because she was very particular about dust. In minus 40 degrees she would open all the doors every morning to sweep the floor. I used to hate that.

We had an outside toilet that was about one hundred feet away from home. Korean people say "the toilet and in-laws must be distant." Most homes had remote toilets. Our toilet was so huge that I called it the toilet house.

We lived in the same village with our father for a while, but we were a half mile apart from each other except the first and the tiny house we lived in were on the same property. For some reason we switched houses with my father several times. Later I remember my father lived in another house (let me call it No. 3 house). That house was on the way to my school. I used to pick up a newspaper from my father's box in town on the way home from school and drop it off at his place, which I used to pass to and from school. There was no school in our village until my father donated a piece of land to build a grade school. Until then, we walked two and half miles to go to school. For a young first grader it was very far on foot.

There was a time he moved away to another town a few miles away from us, and we lived in the No. 3 house he used to live in. I remember living in three houses of the four. We never lived in house No. 4, which was in the peach orchard. An old steward who took care of the orchard always lived there.

I didn't have any girls growing up around me. There were several boys. One of them was very mean. I don't know any other boys' names but his because he was so mean to me. His great-grandmother used to babysit for me while my mother was out of the village and he gave me hard time. I used to hate him.

When I grew up I didn't have any girls' play. Most time I had boys' sports. In winter we used to slide on the ice or on the snow. We didn't have anything like skis. I used to carry a small pillow on my back as my doll; My mother would put it on my back, wrapping around it with a thin cover and tying it with wide cloth string. That was a doll for me. In those days there were no dolls except pillow dolls. After she married my brother, my sister-in-law made a very tiny, finger-size doll for me.

We were so rich that I envied poor people's food. My mother would let me carry rice in a metal bowl, tie it on my back just like my pillow doll. I would carry it to our neighbors and ask for their food. They seldom had white rice but had barley, millet, or plain clams. Nowadays these are healthy foods, but in those days, only the rich could eat white rice.

CHAPTER 4

Liberation to Oppression

August 15, 1945 when World War II ended, I was ten years old. At the time, we lived in No. 3 house. I remember my brother Chin Ho was listening to his old-style radio to hear the Japanese king's surrender speech. Korea regained her independence from the Japanese occupation. We got our own names, language, national anthem, and flag back. However, before our tears of joy over our new independence were dry, the Russian communist regime settled in the northern side of the country and Americans began to show up in the southern part. Thus, Korea has been divided up to this date and the two parts remain everlasting enemies. In school, the Japanese national anthem was replaced by a North Korean song, "General Kim, Il Sung." We had to learn to sing that every day.

We lived in the country home a short while longer and then we moved back to Ham Heung City, my birthplace. My brothers built a house there. I was transferred to another grade school located in the Hwang Keum Jung area. It was the central area of Ham Heung City.

For some reason, perhaps because an income source was there, my mother took me and Chin Woo back to the No. 3 house in Sun Duck village. We lived there for little while again. There, Russian soldiers often showed up asking for apples and eggs. I couldn't let my sister-in-law appear before those guys. In those days, young women were easily raped by Russian soldiers. I wanted to protect her. I hid her inside the house and I would appear before them asking what they wanted. I gave them a bag full of apples and boiled their eggs as they demanded and sent them off.

My sister-in-law was pregnant and her due date was coming closer. The day she was having delivery pain, I cooked potatoes and gave them to her. I picked well-ripened peaches and brought them to her to eat. My mother helped her to deliver the baby, Young Soo. That was August 15, 1946, at 2:15 p.m.

Forced Labor

At the tender age of ten I went out to the labor field representing my family. I took on the responsibility, sensing that no one else from my family would do it. Every family was forced to do labor work for the community—road work or sowing rice plants in the muddy rice field. They used to work for my father and accepted me because they knew him. With my frail ten-year-old frame I carried a little basin filled with dirt on my head to a designated spot where I would dump it. I also had to learn how to sow rice plants in the muddy fields with my bare feet.

Escape for Life

After we lived there a little while, my brother Chin Ho took off to South Korea when he realized that he couldn't survive under the communists' persecution for being highly educated and the eldest son of a wealthy man; their persecution was and is mean and violent up to this day. I think that was 1946. Too many educated and wealthy people were violently slain. At the time Chin Ho's wife was carrying a baby. As part of the highly educated wealthy class, my family was at risk of being punished on top of having lost all our land and crops. As a child I heard that some of my father's wealthy and educated colleagues were beaten to death. I also heard that North Korean communists were persecuting defeated remnant Japanese stationed in North Korea; If they couldn't escape fast enough they were slain. All the farm land was taken away from my father too. Three houses and orchards remained with us until we left. They spared my father's life though. I heard the reason was that he did good in the community and for his workers. I could tell that was true by his workers' behavior after all our farm land was taken away, leaving no crops for us to survive. The village people who worked for my father secretly brought us rice in the night, lest anyone see them. No wonder they accepted me, a ten-year-old child with light labor to represent my family and recorded that my family participated in the labor work.

Thus, the land was covered in dark clouds although we gained our independence and freedom from the thirty-six-year-long Japanese occupation. This was an ordeal of one year in North Korea (August 1945 to Spring 1947) for me. Except for our abusive father, the rest of us escaped to South Korea because my oldest brother was at risk of being arrested. We made the getaway two by two. Even though we owned vast land and orchards, we left North Korea with empty hands, with no cash in our pockets. We couldn't carry lands, orchards, or crops on our back. Each one of us had just one backpack on our back for we each faced many days of walking in hiding since crossing the border was illegal then under communist rule. At the time, we had no option but to risk our lives by seeking freedom in South Korea. Somehow my second-oldest brother and I were the last to leave North Korea in the fall of 1947. He was nineteen and I was eleven. So, he and I were under the North Korean regime for one more year before we made our escape to South Korea. With a long-drawn iron curtain and land mines under the ground, we were permanently separated from our abusive farther and other relatives in North Korea forever. We still don't know why our father didn't escape. Therefore, in my first ten years of life, I had already experienced plenty of homelessness according to my definition of homelessness: physical, emotional, social and spiritual.

PART TWO

Homelessness in Freedom: Freedom in Homelessness

CHAPTER 5

Bone-Piercing Poverty

When my brother, Chin Woo and I arrived in Seoul on foot, it resembled Ham Heung City but in a child's eyes it looked larger with more lights and neon signs. My brother knew where to find my other family members, whom we soon joined.

Our father had never given us enough cash while we were in North Korea. We couldn't bring any property in our backpack. Suddenly we became refugees in our own country, falling into poverty, and began to experience cold, hunger and homelessness, constantly moving from a temporary room to two rooms. For my elder brother, who was then the head of the household, found it hard to find a room for six of us.

Today when I hear a homeless friend ask me to find a room for such a large family I gasp because I know how hard it is even in the U.S. today. Then I can relate to the difficulty that my brother Chin Ho must have had to face in those days.

Thus, we exchanged freedom from persecution in the north with hunger, cold and homelessness in South Korea. But it was still better than North Korea because we had no fear of being arrested and condemned. I hear such a story a lot from homeless friends who ran away from abusive parents. They say they'd rather live in peace and freedom in homelessness than fear and abuse, especially abuse of a physical or sexual nature. Not knowing what this means, the public easily says "they chose to be homeless and therefore, there is no room for our sympathy for them."

My brothers and my mother tried to get jobs. It wasn't easy but my brother, Chin Ho, got a job as an English interpreter for an American-owned hotel. While he was in high school and college in Japan he studied

English very hard. When I was very young, I used to play with his English vocabulary cards and got into trouble. This means I was exposed to English words very early on. This might have contributed to my interest many decades later in this language and culture. My mother, at one time, got a temporary job in the laundry department of the same hotel, which of course didn't last long. Chin Ho had a few friends from his high school—Bo Sung—in Seoul. We rented rooms from their houses temporarily. Friends couldn't tolerate such a large family for long time and we were frequently told to vacate room(s) and had to face one housing crisis after another. This is the story of many of my homeless friends today. We never could get over our housing problem because we were a large family, and there was not enough housing for hundreds of thousands of refugees from North Korea who fled just like us from the communists' persecution, which still goes on to this day. The irony is that my homeless friends who do not live under the communists' persecution and aren't refugees experience the same circumstances in their own free, loving, and democratic country.

Spring in Seoul

In Seoul, our first winter was so cold. Temperature there were supposed to be higher than in North Korea, where it usually goes down to minus 40 degrees. But soon spring came around with flowers blooming, not just in our environment but in our hearts as well. Even in wartime a new life gets to be born and in time of chaos and struggle something good can come up if we wait with patience. A sort of a rosebud was coming up through the trash piles.

Grade School

After moving around from room to room for a while we rented a two-bedroom apartment in the Don Am Dong area and enrolled me in the fourth grade at Don Am Elementary School. Up until then I couldn't enroll in any school. I started out as a good student. Boys and girls followed me to my apartment to be friends with me. At another point we moved away to the opposite end of the city from where I needed to take two different streetcars to go to school. Instead of transferring to different neighborhood school, I decided to remain at Don Am Elementary despite the distance. When breakfast and my lunch box weren't ready, I just left home for school. When I arrived at school there was no child in school. I was the first one. I earned double awards with academic achievement and perfect attendance. Even when I was sick I would go to school. I didn't miss a day. My mother and brothers had never required me to do this. Early on I guess I was a workaholic and wanted to be a perfect student.

Chin Ho Enlisted in the Korean Army

Chin Ho heard that if he joined the Korean Army he would get free housing for seven of us. Six of us crossed the border but we are now seven because a baby boy (Chul Soo) came along to Chin Ho and his wife. So he joined a special class of the Ninth Korean Army Academy and his army ID number was 16339. Chin Ho once told me his number and I never forgot. After getting training, he earned the rank of lieutenant and was stationed in the Yong San Korean Army compound. Later this became the Eighth U.S. Army compound. He got a free two-bedroom apartment. We didn't have to worry about moving around or how to get rent money anymore. He was a national soccer player and a good singer, so he was well accepted in the army, I heard. Now I know that the poor go to war. If we hadn't had housing problems, he wouldn't have joined the army at the age of twenty-nine.

Bonding

While I was growing up in South Korea in my brother's household (from age eleven to fifteen) he used to ask me to tend his baby, Young Soo, my nephew. I used to carry him on my back every day before and after school while my sister-in-law was busy with housework. Young Soo used to wet my back as perhaps I did on his father's back in my infancy. Since we didn't have good diapers in those days, babies had frequent accidents anywhere and everywhere. So both he and his brother, Chul Soo, grew up with me. In later years, I took them to church. They were in the Sunday school class I taught. They went anywhere I went with me.

An Irony: Ewah Girls' Junior High School

The Girl in the Color Purple went to a prestigious private high school in Korea. In 1949, I signed up to go to a public junior high school, which was cheaper and second class among schools at the time. But my homeroom teacher suggested I take an admission test for Ewah Girls' Junior High School, which was the most prestigious private junior and senior high school in Korea. The competition was so high that grade school kids studied like PhD candidates. At the time I hadn't a clue about the sky-high tuition for this institution. I took the entrance exam as the teacher suggested and passed all the tests. I can still recall my mother and my eldest brother having mixed emotions; they were elated for me that I passed, but sad that they could not pay for my high tuition. They tried and tried but couldn't come up with the full amount of the tuition. My eldest brother, an army officer then, went to see the school principal and told him that my family couldn't pay the full tuition. To everyone's surprise, the school principal accepted my enrollment with what we had—half the amount of tuition. He was the first Christian I encountered, and my first taste of Christ's spirit. The school was a mission school built by American Methodist Missionaries, and it turned my life around from one with no Jesus to one with Jesus. From that day on I seemed to be destined to live in the Spirit of God.

I had only a pair of school uniforms and wore torn tennis shoes. I walked two miles to school every day. Many Ewah Girls' came in sedans owned by their parents wearing shiny leather shoes, which was very rare in those days. Many girls came from bank CEO fathers, government officer fathers, and business fathers. But nothing discouraged me. Even at this early age, I had a purpose in life to get a good education and become independent, as my mother's credo emphasized. And finally, I got into school, the best school in Korea, which Chin Ho used to promise he would help me do. I was only honored. There was no room for discouragement.

During that first year I was in my new school a few friends of mine invited me to church. I tried a few times but I wasn't interested in them. I got a headache when preachers shouted in preaching. I was going in and out of the church for the sake of a friend. That was the level of my faith in the first year.

PART THREE

Korean War
Chon Shin Man Ko

CHAPTER 7

War and Homelessness

While we were going through four years of deadly struggle to survive in South Korea, suddenly, the North Korean Army invaded us. It was Sunday morning, June 25, 1950, and I was fifteen. We were living in my brother's army apartment. On that Sunday, Chin Ho put civilian clothes on, and went out to have a good time with his friends. Who would imagine that would be the last time I saw him. He left his twenty-seven-year-old wife and two little boys. He was thirty then.

That day, his wife and I visited Yong San Korean Army compound. Hardly anyone was there anymore. They were all either gone to the battlefield or had left Seoul already. On the way home, we had to constantly hide ourselves from the fighter jet flying low over our heads making a horrible loud noise.

Han River Bridge was cut off already. Government officials did that after they got out of Seoul city. The rest of us were trapped in the city. Han River Bridge was the main bridge to get to the South.

Within three days, uninvited and unwanted Communist Army tanks rolled into Seoul. We couldn't stay at the army housing because we were at risk of being arrested. We were hiding from possible execution by the Communist Occupation Forces because we were North Korean refugees and a South Korean Army family. We burned all of Chin Ho's army clothes to get rid of all the traces of his life as a South Korean Army officer.

One day, my second-oldest brother, Chin Woo, was arrested by the North Korean army. But he somehow escaped. Immediately my mother sent him and I to the countryside where Chin Ho's friend from the same home village in North Korea was living. We walked. It took two days on foot to get there. But it wasn't any safe place because the house we were supposed to stay in was right by the railroad station. Communist soldiers stop there on the way to and from their destination. They brought us rice to cook for them. We did it. They would leave a bowl of rice for Chul Soo, Chin's Ho's two-year-old baby, who was so sick and thin, his legs were twisted skin and bones and he looked like he was near death. But my brother, Chin Woo, couldn't be visible at all because they would take him back to the battlefield. So we dug a hole in the kitchen and covered it up with bushes and firewood. He stayed in that hole with an English dictionary, eating a little food we gave him.

I had to make a living as a fifteen-year-old girl. I followed country women who took rice to Seoul city to sell and bring different items and then exchanged them for crops or potatoes in the country. I did the same thing. My mother exchanged her clothes for twenty-five pounds of rice. I would carry it on my head to Seoul. We walked for two days on foot, sleeping on the road since it was summer. I would exchange rubber shoes. It was equally heavy. Both ways, I would carry them on my head or on my back. It was too heavy to carry by hand. My mother took them around to exchange or barley or potatoes. When I arrived home, for a few days I couldn't stand on my feet or walk because both legs and ankles were hurting so bad that I had to crawl. I made four such trips, which means eight trips in total (or sixteen days of walking). Perhaps that is the reason I stopped growing and stayed short.

We struggled to survive this way until September 28, 1950. U.N and U.S. shot rockets or bombs from Inchon Shore toward Seoul to chase the Communist Army out of the city. September 28 happened to be the date of my fourth such business trip to Seoul. I was in the central area of Seoul with my relative that night. The whole city was on fire, including the house right next door. I had to run out of the house screaming "Fire!" to wake my relatives up. Millions of people were in the streets that night because too many houses were burning. Some people were shot by enemies running away. It was chaos!

In the morning, after running around on the streets all night escaping bombing and burning, I went to see what happened to the temporary hut we had been hiding in. On the way I had to cross so many bodies to get there. Everything burned down there too. I had never seen so many bodies in my whole life—bodies of children, men, and women and some so burned that gender was indiscernible. That night Seoul was recovered from the communist occupation by U.N Forces. But we the civilians were bombed by both sides—U.N. forces and the retreating communists.

CHAPTER 8

Exile

For October, November, December, we had hope that we would win the war because the U.N. and the Korean Army were able to push forward to North Korea. However, suddenly we heard news that a huge Chinese army had joined the North Korean Army. The U.N. began to retreat from their frontline in North Korea because they didn't want to risk World War III. Eventually they withdrew. Citizens and even schoolchildren like us cried out for them to finish up the war.

The communists and the Chinese kept pushing us southward and finally on January 4, 1951, now known as "One-Four Retreat," we had to vacate Seoul again. It was the second time we were defeated. Army families were notified this time to go into exile to the most southern part of the country. As instructed, we all went out to the Seoul train station. Too many people were already there trying to get on the train heading to Pusan. It was so crowded that we couldn't get through the doors and had to go through the windows. Inside the train already looked like a can of sardines. Many people got on top of the train and hung on to the doors. From Seoul to Pusan is a four-hour trip today. That day it took twelve days. One elderly woman fell off the train, severing one of her legs above the knee. I didn't even know if she was taken to the hospital in that chaos and if she made it. Train stopped or started without warning anywhere they wanted. When they stopped everyone got off and cooked rice outside the train. When they started again without warning, everyone got back on with hot pots. It was an unimaginable chaotic, anxiety-stricken scene!

When the six of us (Chin Woo, my mother, sister-in-law and her two boys, and myself) got off at Pusan Jin train station, there was no place to go. My brother and mother looked for a room. But *there was no room at the inn for us.* Millions of people rushed into that little port city. There was neither food nor drinking water available. Pusan, our city of exile, wasn't welcoming us at all. The wealthy ones already rented rooms and those who had relatives in Pusan got rooms also. Strangers like us had no help. There was neither welfare service nor social worker. Darkness fell on us. We had to doze off in the parking lot of a train station for three nights, having the cold concrete ground as our bed and the sky as our ceiling.

It was December, winter in Korea. Every day we looked for a room or water. There was none. Three days later, an old man invited us into his yard to sleep. There we created a little tent with our bed sheets first and then turned it into an 8x8 tiny house with ration boxes and whatever we could grab. There were other families doing the same thing with us. In winter, we would warm up a rock, wrap it with clothes, put it in the middle of the room, and cover it with a comforter and everyone put their feet in there and went to sleep. The rock heated our feet and our bodies heated one another. It wasn't even big enough for one person but we appreciated such minimal life. In our hometown in North Korea we moved around between our own three houses and never lacked anything except freedom.

Me on the Young Do Island.

My mother had a little peddler shop on the streets. She and I got up at 4 a.m. because there was a competition for the good spots on the street corners. She had cigarettes, gum, chocolates, and a few other items on her counter. I would go to the black market to buy U.S.-made items for her to sell.

Ewah Girls' Junior and Senior High School started on Young Do Island in tents. Chairs were planted on the ground for us to sit on. No tables. One hundred and twenty third-year girls packed in one tent class, the only one for that grade.

One thing we all will never forget is our English teacher. His name was Mr. Bong Kook Lee, and he was very gentle and nice, but a tough teacher. In his class, his speed was so fast that we could hardly breathe. We had to memorize English vocabulary in our sleep, and while walking on the street. Years later we all appreciate this teacher. Because of him, we all acquired English grammar. We couldn't speak, though. The grammar I still remember is what I learned from him in my mid-teen years.

I didn't go to church while in exile for three years. Lately, I began to wonder why, and asked my girlfriend when I saw her recently in Los Angeles. She used to take me to church in the first year at Ewah, but I wondered why she didn't invite me to church in Pusan exile. She said she did, but I refused to go. I was too busy making a living.

My mother made me a desk with wooden apple box, covering the top with newspaper. That was the only furniture in tiny 8x8 box house. But I was a good student. Except for helping my mother with her little peddler shop, all I did was study.

And my brother, Chin Woo, went to another city to find a job. He worked and saved some money. My sister-in-law, Chin Ho's wife, cooked octopus and sold them at the train station parking lot to travelers since when travelers get off the train early in the morning many were hungry and would eat them.

While we were in Pusan I got on a train and visited the Korean Army headquarters in Taegu, Korea. I asked the officers what had happened to my brother. They had a record of him as "missing in action." His colleague there changed his status from "missing" to "deceased" so his family could get a pension during the war. From 1951 up to her last breath in August of 2018 my sister-in-law received his death benefit from the Korean government. Of course, we never saw Chin Ho after June 25, 1950, so she deserves to get his death benefit.

We stayed in Pusan for three years until the war ended in 1953. Korean history remembers that General MacArthur wanted to end the war, just as Korean people wanted, but President Truman fired MacArthur and negotiated a truce with North Korea. We heard it was because the U.S. didn't want to fight with China. Well, after killing several million people in both North and South Korea and 58,000 U.S. soldiers the war stopped where it started achieving nothing.

CHAPTER 9

Coming Home from Exile

In 1953 the armistice was signed between the two Koreas. Ever since the ceasefire, we have lived in fear of yet another war, even to the present day.

In the winter of 1953, we were able to return to Seoul from our three-year exile. We didn't have our home in Seoul anymore because it was burned in the war. We lived temporarily in someone's empty house with no heat, in the dead of winter. The winter in Pusan was mild but it was bitter cold in Seoul. Living in a house with no heat left all of my fingers frostbitten.

Once back in Seoul, I went back to Ewah Girls' High School, which reopened on the original campus in Cheong Dong, Seoul. Again, I was the poorest child in the whole school. I never had a regular winter Ewah uniform of high-quality fabric in a navy-blue color. Mine was the top of a woman's soldier uniform dyed in dark-navy color with white Ewah collar. I only had one winter school uniform and one summer uniform. I had to wash and dry it overnight to wear it the next morning. I never wore shiny leather shoes as the other Ewah Girls' did. Mine were old sneakers with holes, but I was never ashamed. I only concentrated on my studies.

All of my troubled early life makes me liken myself to the poor/homeless I serve today because my story is their story and vice versa.

I was happy to return to school and continue my studies. I was in my second year of high school now. My brother, Chin Woo, tried to support my tuition. Despite our poverty, hunger, and frequent moving, I studied hard. On the way home from school, when I ran into him in Myung Dong, the busiest central business section of Seoul, he used to take me to a Western or Chinese restaurant. I enjoyed eating fried pork steak. I remember he used to bring me brand-new bills to pay my tuition. Later, tuition got so high that he couldn't afford it anymore. Ewah gave me the Kang Hee Scholarship. Kang Hee is the name of the daughter of the then vice president of Korea. She died when she was one class above me. Her father gave Ewah the sum of money, enough to cover all her tuition had she lived. Many girls including me got Kang Hee Scholarship. To this date, I appreciate it.

This vice president and his wife were later shot to death by their own son, who also killed himself after slaying his parents. They ended their life this way in a politically difficult situation to which they reportedly contributed. But they did something good for the future students. They are all dead, including their little daughter, but the scholarship is well and alive to this day, and I am one of the beneficiaries. We will all die, but our giving, in whatever form, be it money, vision, ideal, or service, will keep on living as Kang Hee lives on forever!

The Casualties of the Korean War Were too Heavy

In the three-year Korean War, an estimated 3 million Koreans died, and killed nearly 1 million Chinese troops. According to the U.S./Defense Casualty Analysis System, the U.S. lost almost 34,000 service members and more than 105,000 were wounded. Other sources report that the U.S. lost 58,000 lives in combat and non-combat circumstances. Blair, Leckie, and the *Encyclopedia Americana* cite Pentagon estimates for the total killed, wounded and missing: All U.N.: 996,937; South Korea: 850,000; All communists: 1,420,000; China: 900,000; North Korea: 520,000.

Massive destruction, millions of lives of Koreans and U.N. soldiers, and widows, orphans, beggars, homeless elderly, severe poverty and everlasting wounds and grief, and hatred were the products of the Korean War. Any war, in my opinion, achieves nothing. It only destroys and kills. Why do we have a war? War is deadly sin. Whoever causes war is committing unforgivable sin because it takes away God-given precious lives and destroys the God-blessed world.

Before he realized his dream for me, my brother, Chin Ho, was killed in the Korean War in 1951. I was deeply wounded and so was my mother and his wife and two young sons (Young Soo and Chul Soo). The whole family, along with million others, wept for many years. Chin Ho was my father figure, whom I loved dearly and depended on. My mother grieved for her son till her last breath. So, the war and exile were Chon Shin Man Ko (a thousand pains and ten thousand troubles) and homelessness.

As we left our beloved homes, neighbors, and friends, I learned what it means to lose everything we owned. Did I ever dream that I would work with homeless women and men later, who had lost everything, being evicted from their familiar environment and be in a strange place that was like foreign country within their own country? This experience helps me feel at home with stories of Jesus's human parents escaping with him when he was a baby to Egypt and the Israelites who escaped Egypt from Pharaoh's oppression. Did God prepare me to work with those who run for freedom in my later years?

PART FOUR

God Came Into My Life

CHAPTER 10

I Found God at Ewah

In exile in Pusan, I didn't go to church at all. However, back in Seoul, my faith in Jesus was ignited. In hopeless times God visits us but we often do not realize it. Ewah was and is a mission school that is operated by Christian spirits. We had a chapel service every morning before the first class, which we started with prayer. Teachers were very friendly and gracious. They educated girls to be open, cheerful, and serving the society.

In those days, girls' high schools allowed one hair style. But Ewah allowed two styles—braid or short cut to suit each girl. I tried both styles.

I liked the Bible class taught by the then Bishop of the Methodist Church. He was an angel. I got 100 percent on the Bible test and faithfully attended the morning service at the school chapel. I ended up joining a Christian students group in school, and quickly became a leader of my class. I was even baptized by the same bishop at the school chapel. That was the first time God came into my life, at eighteen. In my late-teen years, I became profoundly attracted to the image of Jesus; who was poor and homeless and walked among people like himself.

Jean with a leader from the school's Christian Students Group, in which I became very active.

We had a visiting woman preacher, Ms. Kang Sung Il, now and then for our chapel. I fell in love with her. I wanted to grow up like her. Along with Bible class, chapel, and her preaching I got really interested in God. Suddenly my heart was burning for God. I attended chapel with much interest. Ewah made me a Christian. But the first girl that took me to church was Young Soon Cho. I also attended the neighborhood church, which was Presbyterian, and became very faithful to the church

that I attended on Sundays. At school I was Methodist. At home I was Presbyterian. I didn't know the difference. I joined the high school class at church and served as vice president and secretary. As a high school kid, I became a Sunday school teacher.

The photo is my Sunday School class. Two of my deceased brother's kids are there.

Along with a friend of mine, I rented a room in Kang Sung Il's neighborhood. Every evening we visited her, talked with her, and looked at her. In her later years as an old maid, she married a man. One day, in my seminary years, I visited her, and she was sick in bed. She might have been pregnant. It is sad that I don't recall telling her that I wanted to be like her. I wish I did. I hope I did. But I don't remember telling her. She was someone who deeply influenced me.

One time I was selected by the gym teacher to be in an athletic team for short-distance running and long jump. But practice every day after school interfered with my studies. I quit, and the gym teacher wasn't happy at all.

Wearing the white summer gym uniforms of the girls' high school. I'm in the front row (right).

Calling

For our graduation, all the other girls chose a fancy place to take their class picture, such as a park or a palace, but I let my group take a picture of us singing from a hymnal and reading the Bible. The picture below shows just how very old-fashioned and odd it was to do that, even in that period.

Life Path Dawned in Prayer Service

I experienced my first mysterious calling: in the last quarter of my last year in high school, in the winter of 1954, our home church started a 100-day dawn prayer service.

Photo taken from my yearbook: I am the second from the left, kneeling and leading singing.

My prayer at the time was asking God what college I should go to. The answer to my prayer didn't come until toward the end of the 100-day prayer meeting. One early morning while I was praying, my heart was telling me to go to a theological seminary. All along, my family had been urging me to go to either a medical or law school. They had the distorted idea that I was a brilliant girl. Studying

Wearing the dark-navy winter uniforms with white collars. Far left is me.

theology was completely contrary to their wish for me. When they learned about my vision, they were all shocked and grieved as if I were dead. This was my first awakening to God's calling at eighteen. The church leaders, however, loved to hear the news, and guided me to go to a seminary.

To this day, I deeply appreciate Ewah for giving me an education and guidance to Christian faith. I am who I am today because of Ewah. The spirit of my social service for the poor is all rooted in Ewah Spirit.

Photo is taken after practice of our athletic group. I am on the far left in front row.

Seminary Education

The girl who didn't want to go to church in Pusan, now ended up going to seminary. What a turnaround! So I took the entrance exam at the Han Kuk Theological Seminary, a Korean Presbyterian seminary. I was told that my English test score was good. A graduate of Ewah, a top class private high school, was welcomed to the seminary. Some theology courses were difficult to understand but I always got a good grade. In German language class we took six tests in a semester; I got six perfect scores. I was known as a smart girl. I didn't understand much of my systematic theology course, but my test score was ninety-eight. In seminary years, I wasn't very active with school extracurricular programs. I didn't join any volunteer service either. The only thing I was interested in was studying. But this doesn't mean I studied all the time. I would get up at 3 a.m. and study. I went to bed at 10 p.m.

Graduation and Study Abroad in the U.S.

When the time to graduate came closer I heard a rumor that I was second in my class and another male student was to get the top honor. I visited the Dean's office and requested to calculate my scores again because I couldn't believe I wasn't the top student.

1959, the day I was graduating from Han Shin Seminary with the highest honors.

They did, discovered that I had the highest scores, and corrected the mistake. To this day, it is a mystery where the mistake came from. I can't seem to stop thinking that they preferred that a male student get the first prize.

However, I graduated in 1959 summa cum laude.

Many people were so excited that it was the first time ever a woman got the first prize in the seminary history. As the photo shows, Dr. Tae Young Ham, who was the former vice president of Korea and an honorary president of our seminary handed the certificates to me and Jeong Cheol Nam, and he had to sit down because he was so fragile and elderly that he couldn't be on his feet too long.

On the commencement day, an unknown American female missionary who attended the event hugged me by opening her arms and whole heart to congratulate me because "a woman got it." But I was a little sorry for the male classmate who had expected to be the first.

Many decades later, when I was working on my doctor of ministry degree at San Francisco Theological Seminary I ran into this male student (Jeong Cheol Nam), at a Han Shin Seminary alumni gathering in San Francisco. He was an old man who didn't recognize me, and I didn't recognize him either. As I was walking in to the room where he was waiting for us, he kept asking, "Which one is Jean Kim?" Once we recognize each other we were very happy to be reconnected. He told me that he had married a wealthy woman and was operating a liquor store in San Francisco. I felt sorry for him again when I heard him saying he was not happy. Several years ago, I heard he passed away. I felt sorry for him again. He could have done something great since he was a bright man.

This experience in gender discrimination in church motivated me in later years to help the National Council of the Korean Presbyterian Church (NCKPC-PC/USA) set up a special study committee that was developed into the Women's Leadership Committee for the whole Korean Presbyterian Church (U.S.A.) to help enhance women's ordination as leaders in Korean Presbyterian churches in the U.S.

It was the most honorable day for me. My mother participated in the event, but I missed my eldest brother on that day very much. I got my bachelor's in divinity and another bachelor's in English literature after that from another college in Korea.

When I graduated from the seminary, I decided to be a social worker for the most marginalized, modeling my life after Jesus, who sat with, ate with, talked with, walked with, accepted, and healed the poor, hungry, sick, homeless, women, children, and outcasts of his time. This image of Jesus had captured me early on in my teen years.

The first year, I worked for the Christian Children's Fund in Korea and later for CARE-Korea. I decided not to become a Biblical linguistic scholar, as some of my seminary professors suggested. I quickly discovered that I would have to change my role as leading student in the seminary to a second-class position in the Korean church system because of my gender. Women couldn't be ordained, and had to stand behind a male pastor as his subordinate. I refused to be treated as an inferior, second-class human being, so I became a social worker instead.

University of Chicago Divinity School

Studying abroad was every talented student's aspiration in those days. My ambition to study abroad was deep in my soul, as my eldest brother had implanted the idea in me early on. In 1960, I took an exam to study abroad. Passing the national exam was like passing the bar exam by today's standards. I passed once again and was able to attend the University of Chicago Divinity School for one year. Unfortunately, however, I had to return to Korea because my scholarship ended. I promised myself I would return someday. I can still remember Dr. Marcus Barth who was the son of Karl Barth loaned me his book because I couldn't hang on to a library book for too long.

So three events were the highlights for me in those days: getting into **Ewah Girls'** Junior High School, graduating with **summa cum laude** honors from seminary, and passing the **national exam for students going abroad**. I had achieved my mother's credo.

CHAPTER 12

A Few Stories to Tell

I remember being loved by most seminary professors but particularly the Reverend Dr. Chung Choon Kim. It was an era when Korean church leaders wanted to be mature leaders by leaving the control of American missionaries.

One day, Dr. Kim asked me to go somewhere with him. It was the day Korean Churches were gathering at the Sung Nam Presbyterian Church building, which he was serving as a pastor. He didn't seem to want to participate in the protest of Korean Churches against the missionaries' control. Korean pastors were saying "we (Korean Churches) are over age fifty and no longer need parental protection or control." He took me to the outskirt of Seoul. We sat on the bank between rice fields and killed time by talking for several hours, returning when the meeting was over.

Photo of me with the Reverend Dr. Chung Choon Kim on the seminary campus in late 1950s).

Another was professor Oo Jung Lee, who taught us English and Greek. I used to attend senior class for reading English theological texts. She gave me a 105 score instead of 100 because, she said, my test results were more than perfect and deserved 105.

Another experience was with Professor Ik Hwan Moon who taught us Hebrew. I did well with that also. But one time I had a surgery, which meant I had to skip the test. I asked him to allow me to take the test by myself alone later when I was recovered from the surgery. He denied that request and instead divided the scores from my previous three tests (300) by four to include the one I missed.

So on my seminary transcript I have one score of seventy-five recorded. I'll never forget that frustrating experience.

PART FIVE

Dark Purple Life

Marriage and Children

To make a long, complicated story short, my brother Chin Woo and my mother never wanted me to marry this man because he was the same age as my oldest brother. It was my first marriage. But he was a divorced man. Perhaps I wanted to experience the love and care that my brother used to offer me, and I might have been replacing his love. This man deeply loved me. But my family grieved just as they did when I went to seminary, because they felt I should have married a younger man. He was ready to give up his life if hadn't married him.

So we got married. Two children, Hyoung Soo and Yong Soo (Sam), came along. Our dark purple life started: As my family worried, I became a bread earner. My husband was so

Our wedding day

highly educated—with two college degrees—he was often overqualified and couldn't get a job. He wanted to be a lawmaker but there weren't any openings. So he did lots of volunteer work with not much income to bring bread to the table.

Homelessness

Throughout the ten years of our married life in Korea we were very poor, moved every single year, from room to room. Moving ten times in a ten year period was a very difficult thing to do with kids. It was an experience of homelessness.

Me and my husband with my oldest son Hyoung Soo

Whenever I meet my homeless sisters who had made bad choices with the wrong man and ended up being poor, suffering from financial and housing troubles, I say "yes, don't I know all about it? It is my own story, sisters." But I never gave up living fully at my best.

At one point, we were living in a house we had rented before Sam was born in Koo Ro Dong, which was quite far from the city. As soon as I got home from the hospital with the new baby, a gas leak in the new house nearly killed me. At the time, all houses used gas heat, but often it leaked through tiny holes. Fortunately, I got the brunt of the gas and Sam was okay. Before the house killed anyone, we moved back to the city.

My youngest son Sam

From the start, Sam was such a good baby. He would go to sleep with me at 10 p.m. and wake up at 6 a.m., my rising time. Because I worked, his schedule was so helpful that I called him my "savior." My husband was so irresponsible financially that I wanted to teach him a lesson or divorce him. I discussed it with the landlady, who understood my troubles. She agreed to care for my children until the evening when their father came home. My oldest boy was four and baby Sam was less than a year old. I gave Hyoung money to go to the store and buy candy for himself. While he was gone, I left home with a suitcase. I hid myself in a center for women, which was like the YWCA's women's quarters of today. Someone got me an English tutor job for a wealthy family.

Later I heard that my husband, immediately checked my mother's home when he learned that I'd left him. He brought the kids there hoping my mother would find me for them. I didn't tell her at all what I was going to do. I'm not sure how many months I lived with that wealthy family who understood what I was doing. The landlady shared my story with her friend, who happened to know my husband and informed him where I was. He caught me and I had to go home. He was always saying that if I left he would destroy our lives. Under enormous stress, I went back home but I knew something unfortunate could come.

When I look back, I wasn't qualified to be a mother. I only seemed to care about my own unbearable stress. Having grown up as the youngest child who had never taken any big responsibility it was very difficult for me to be the bread winner, a mother, and a fully responsible adult. Now I feel so much guilt to both children. I don't deserve their forgiveness. Even today, I have heartache for hurting my children like that. Was I an idiot or an abuser? Unforgivable!

I have never talked about this experience with my children because it is too painful even to think about it. Before the end of my life comes, I need to be honest and let Sam know how sorry I am and what a bad mother I was. As I write this I feel heartache. Did I love them? Yes, very much. But I was so overwhelmed by hardship and stress that I couldn't handle it. I should have done better, though. I'm not talking about excuses. I'm not asking for forgiveness, because I don't deserve it. Therefore, the day I die it will be called "Happy Day" because finally I will be free from these pains.

CHAPTER 14

Dark Life in Kimpo

Life in Bal San Dong with children was Chon Shin Man Ko Homeless Life; Rev. Choo Shik Lee, a friend of ours, invited us to come help his church and live in Bal San Dong. So between 1965 and 1970 we lived there near Kimpo airport.

As the photo shows, in the 1960s this was a small village. I had a Chon Shin Man Ko life there; we were first robbed while we were living in a rented old clay home. Then we moved into a tiny unheated structure that looked like storage. In those days we heated the floor of the room by burning two round coals that had holes for air in the fireplace in the kitchen. When I would come home from work, often the coal

Hyoung, Sam and I going to church on Sunday. Dad is taking the photo.

died away. It was extremely hard to restart once it went out. I used to cry when that happened. And we had to use a very primitive and frustrating toilet system. I literally had to deal with shit, which was a new experience for me. I had to walk a mile to get to the bus stop through the wind and snow in winter, which triggered my asthmatic cough and quickly progressed into severe bronchitis. In summer, I walked under the burning hot sun or through the muddy road when it rained.

We got six-year-old Hyoung Soo enrolled in Yang Chon Elementary School. There was no bus from our home to the school and it was about two miles away. Hyoung Soo was always so frustrated, lonely, and angry, and got into fights with other kids. He destroyed some neighbors' vegetables. Of course, we first told him that was not good behavior.

When he didn't make any changes, our discipline was spanking. Now looking back, I regret not understanding the mind of a little child as highly educated parents. For this, I will grieve for the rest of my life. Our younger boy had to stay with the babysitter, the late Yon Ok Lee, a deacon of the church. I owe her a huge thanks to this day. Neither of the boys were happy in that environment.

Economically we were barely making it. My husband was a politician then. He told me that right after graduating from Meiji Law School in Japan, he came back home and re-enrolled in Han Shin Theological Seminary. He didn't choose the opportunity to be a judge or a lawyer like his law school alumni. When he graduated from the seminary, he served a church as a student pastor and was never ordained. With his personality he was determined not to pursue ordination. He went back to the political field, which meant he lost the chance to be a lawyer or a pastor. He became heavily involved with political activities. However, his

Hyoung and Sam

earning was very meager, so I had to be the bread winner.

In my ten years of marriage in Korea we moved ten times. I was sick with the housing issue. If you were not able to buy a house, the next choice was to put down a lump sum deposit for a room and get it back when you leave. If you didn't have the lump sum, you have to rent a room on a monthly basis. In our day, there weren't many apartment styles. We all had to rent a room with or without a meager kitchen. Even on a monthly basis I couldn't keep up with just my salary. Whenever they asked us to vacate the room for their own use, raised the price, or we weren't satisfied, we had to move. Moving on a yearly basis was a heck of a job even though we didn't own much. I was working full time for foreign companies, but I could hardly make it. We were poor but I had never asked my wealthy brother for help. I wanted to make it on my own.

After five years, I had quit my job to undertake the process to return to the United States to finish up my studies. But this time, I didn't get the visa. My husband had been invited by a friend of his to Japan to do some business together. This was when we moved to Bal San Dong. My husband's trip to Japan didn't work out either. So we stayed. I think Hyoung was six and Sam was three. We had a nanny because I had to work.

However, I had to have a partial hysterectomy in 1965. The doctor kept me in the hospital for twelve days. I was also in and out of hospital a lot with chronic asthma every winter, sinus surgery, rectum surgery, etc. When I meet homeless friends, who are always so sick with various causes, first I wonder how in the world a person can be so sick, but then I realize that was me, sick all the time.

CHAPTER 15

Rosebuds in a Trash Pile

Helping Build Haeng Shin Presbyterian Church

Here is an unforgettable story: Once a friend of my husband, Park Do Woon, a graduate from the same seminary we went to, came to my house every weekend asking for help in building a church in his little village. He was serving a little church there as an evangelist. I was seven months pregnant with Sam. I took my husband to visit the U.S. Army in the DMZ area near the border, met the commander, and suggested he do something good for the village while he was serving in Korea. He asked, "Like what?"

Park Do Woon in front of the church the village built

I introduced our friend's vision of building a church. Afterward, the commander called Saturdays "Mrs. Kim Day" because I visited that army compound every Saturday for many months. I was working, and I had time only on Saturdays. In those days, the road was so rough, and the bus was rattling so hard that it could have been harmful to my pregnancy, but I was ignorant and enthused about helping others. God protected me.

U.S. soldiers gave us construction materials such as cement, wood, etc. I heard they brought some of them from their neighbor compounds in another remote area. The people of Haeng Shin Village themselves made cement bricks with materials given by U.S. Army personnel. One day, soldiers took me to a building, and told me to look through the window. There was a brass cross being built. On the ceremonial day, Chaplain and a few officers came with the cross and put it on the altar. The beautiful

handmade cross was dedicated to God, which was an expression of those soldiers' love. My son, Sam, went around to all these places in my womb. I wish Mr. Park Do Woon were still living and could talk about this memorable history of his church. I heard he passed away many years ago.

The following photos bear witness that Haeng Shin Church members, including children, worked hard to make and carry cement bricks to build their own church by their own efforts.

Those elderly members might not be there any longer. The youngsters might all be over fifty years old by now. If they could see this photo, they would feel awesome about this experience.

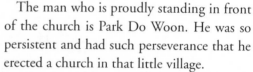

The man who is proudly standing in front of the church is Park Do Woon. He was so persistent and had such perseverance that he erected a church in that little village.

Looking back on those days I feel now that I made an absurd request of these soldiers who were stationed in the deep mountains in the middle of nowhere. It's common sense that they couldn't give away army supplies for such a purpose. But they miraculously agreed to help build a church. It was only the grace of God who moved their hearts to build a house for the Lord so that the poor peasant people in the village could have a place to worship God. No matter how deeply mission-minded these soldiers might have been, without help from God, nothing could have been possible. But with God everything was possible.

It is my witness that God creates something out of nothing and makes the impossible possible. It is my testimony that God presented, participated, intervened, and directed every detail and made things possible. The U.S. Army officials were God's agents!

God has been carrying me on his/her back and landed me where she/he wanted me to work. Reflecting upon things that happened in the past, I am awed how God did it and I thank God for that kind of leadership and making use of me. Therefore, it is God's awesome story.

Now I would like to introduce this story to Haeng Shin Presbyterian Church before it all becomes forgotten history.

The photo is of the cornerstone of the church, which says, *Haeng Shin Presbyterian Church, August 21, 1966.*

Bulldozing a Hill

In the meantime, Rev. Choo Shik Lee, who invited us to live there, wanted to build a church on his hilly lot and ask me to help leveling the hill to make it the church site. How could I level a hill? So one day I visited the U.S. Air Force, which was stationed in Kimpo area. I asked the Air Force commander for a naive and innocent favor to do for a local community. I told him to level the hill so that a church can be built on it. Shortly after our conversation, several soldiers showed up with a bulldozer.

They tried to level the hill but couldn't do it in one day. At the same time, I had an earache that was so bad that I couldn't go to work. I was sick in the house, but now and then I would go out to direct them to level here a little more and there a little more. It took a whole week to level the lot. When they finished their job, my earache ended too. I said, "This is God's story." God moved the heart of the Air Force and God created a chance for me to stay there to work with them. God ended my pain when the job was done. There is no other way to interpret such a happening.

Eventually, they built a church on the lot. When I visited ten years later and worshipped in the church that was built on this bulldozed lot, I wept the whole time in the worship service thinking of my Chon Shin Man Ko life there, my boys, and Rev. Lee.

The Kimpo highway wasn't paved up until the early 1960s. Once it was paved asphalt and became a highway, serious traffic problems arose. Cars ran like bullets and often hit pedestrians. We had to cross the highway to get to the other side of the highway to catch the Seoul-bound bus, just as we did to take our boy to school. We had to cross again

A little hill became a flat lot for the church. As you can see from the photos, the Kimpo area wasn't developed at the time we moved out there.

After bulldozing we enjoyed lunch together with the soldiers that helped level the hill.

in the evening when we came home from work because the bus stopped on the opposite side. We witnessed several serious accidents: One evening many of us got off the bus, stood there and waited for the highway to be clear of traffic. But one woman didn't wait long enough and started to cross. She was hit by a taxi, flying about twenty feet. My husband and taxi driver took her to the hospital, but she died on the way in my husband's arms. She was the mother of three young children. Another time, several of us were standing and waiting for our next bus one morning, when a car hit three girls standing right next to me, throwing them into a ditch by the highway. That time, I took them to a nearby clinic, but they had to be taken to a larger hospital in the city because the local clinic couldn't treat their serious injuries.

Working for the Eighth U.S. Army in Korea

When I came back from the United States in 1962, I worked as an accountant for the PX of the Eighth U.S. Army in Yong San. An American missionary friend introduced me, and I got the job, which was quite unexpected. The first few years I worked all day on a calculator keeping the sales books. Several years later I was promoted to the head cashier's position. This position used to be occupied only by American personnel. My job was to receive all the daily sales money in several bags from forty-one PX stores at the end of the day, and two guns from U.S. Army

Receiving Employee of the Month while working for the 8th Army stationed in Korea.

personnel who carried the money bags. I would store them in a safe. The following morning, I passed these items back to the same people to take them to the bank. And I handled the salaries of the U.S. Army personnel who were connected to the PX and all the Korean staff in our accounting office. There I handled millions of dollars. Every year I had to face two weeks of auditing. They ended it with the comment "best cashier in the world." I learned to do accounting and kept perfect books. At one point, I even got the employee of the month award as the photo shows.

While I was working there I was pregnant with Sam. My American supervisor used to buy me two ice creams saying, "One for you, one for the baby." In the first phase of my pregnancy with Sam I was very sick. I used to run to bathroom, sit on the floor, and throw up into the toilet. We had Western-style flushing toilets at work, which no one had seen in Korea before. At the end of the day, my husband came to get me to take me to a Chinese restaurant because I could hardly eat at all. When we got home, he would stack up many pillows for me to lean my head against so that I wouldn't throw up what I just ate.

Working for CARE- Korea

From 1965 to 1970, I joined CARE-Korea and worked as a social worker to develop a rehabilitation program for twelve leper colonies. My team also helped various orphanages, war widows and elderly people who lost their children in the war. Working for these people was an eye-opening experience to the great need of the poor. And because I was poor, I was able to understand and relate to the people I was helping.

All through the rest of the 1950s and 1960s, we suffered the aftermath of the devastation of the war. I didn't have proper food, clothing, or housing all through my teen years up to my twenties. I believe this is the primary reason I am so short; I didn't have what I needed to grow.

Mission with the Leper Colonies

I went to CARE-Korea, 1965, U.S. social service agency stationed in Korea in post Korean War era. I left a high-paying job as an executive secretary to the CEO of Fairchild, a U.S. company that manufactured transistor radios. They paid well, however, I could see the exploitation, and the inhumane and cold-blooded people. When one of the U.S. personnel drove a twelve-passenger van alone while passing me on the streets, he wouldn't stop to give me a ride despite the freezing cold weather. Perhaps

Interviewing a leper while working with CARE-Korea in the 1960s.

the company had a policy that U.S. personnel shouldn't give rides to Korean staff.

I explained to the CARE staff that I wouldn't work for cold-blooded people for big money. I wanted a job helping the poor like Jesus did. CARE was paying about half of that executive secretary salary, but I accepted the job. First, I was given a job to help TB patients, orphans, widows, and homeless elderly, with medicine and other needed items. I was assigned to develop the CARE rehab program for twelve leper colonies in Kyung Gi Province, which was on the outskirts of the city. My job was to visit the leper colony site, interview people, assess their needs, write a project proposal in English and submit it to New York headquarters. When the New York headquarters approved it, funds came to implement the project. Then I went out, purchased seeds, seedlings, chicks, farm tools, baby pigs, school supplies, etc. for each village to start a self-help project. If we gave them cash, they would eat it up, so I used to deliver these items. The lepers there were inactive cases and weren't contagious, but people didn't want to work with them. The CARE staff discouraged me from accepting that assignment. But I was thinking, "If God wanted me to get leprosy, where could I run from it? But if God protects me no matter where I am, I won't get it. If a theology graduate like me refuses to do this job, who in this world will say yes?" So I made up my mind to carry out the job. CARE had a jeep and driver for official use, which took me to the leper village to do my job.

In that era, people were poor. Bribes were a very common thing. Each organization that received help from CARE brought bribe money to the CARE staff to give them more help. I had never allowed myself to receive a bribe. I told them without a bribe, all the help goes to them anyway. Once, since I knew no bribes, a staff member from the Department of Social and Health Services (DSHS) of the Korean government, who happened to be a Christian and a mission partner with CARE (which gave medication to the DSHS to distribute to tuberculosis patients) brought me a Bible. I had to accept that one.

The eggs we bought hatched into chicks. They grew up and laid eggs. In the fall, they brought me a dozen eggs to show their product. It was amazing to see those eggs as if they were the fruits of my own work. No one wanted those eggs because they came from leper colonies. I ate them all. Since I don't accept bribes, they once invited me out to lunch. That I accepted and ate with them. The CARE staff screamed about that because I ate with lepers. But I really respected and accepted them as Jesus did. What is the difference between them and me? I was fortunate that I didn't get leprosy. That was the only difference. We all are God's children. Who would want to contract leprosy, the most horrible and incurable disease, eating up one's nose and extremities, and leaving a person in horrible physical shape? Looking back, I am glad I served them even in my Chon Shin Man Ko life.

Sometime later CARE promoted me to be in charge of all finances. This position used to be occupied by American personnel. I was dealing with millions of dollars including staff salaries. We had three American staff and ten Korean staff. The Americans were entirely different there. They were very gracious and kind. I felt very comfortable with them. When I left Korea, they gave me very outstanding recommendations to use as references when I looked for a job in the U.S.

I should mention that the Korean government, after the Korean War, couldn't handle the increasing lepers and chased them out to a piece of land in the remote countryside to survive there. CARE-Korea continued to work with the Korean government, giving medication for TB and leprosy and other aid.

Hyoung Goes to the U.S.

As I mentioned earlier, the life of my oldest boy, Hyoung, was very difficult, sharing my Chon Shin Man Ko existence. So I wanted to run to the United States as my refuge and to pursue an advanced study. I sent my oldest boy, age seven, in advance to his aunt in St. Louis, thinking that

my heart would go with him, and my body would join him sooner or later. Perhaps a lot sooner. Joining him would be my huge motivation to leave Korea for good.

So he went to St. Louis ahead of me. I think that was our mistake, not understanding this child. It took longer than I wished for me to join him in the States. He was there about two years before I joined him. First his aunt

Hyoung with his aunt holding him in her arms as he got off the plane in St.Louis.

welcomed him since she had no child of her own and loved her nephew. She sent him to grade school there and cared for him. But several months later, she left him with her sister. Under his other aunt's care, he acted out and got into trouble. In those days we couldn't call him too often, either, because it cost twelve dollars per minute. At one point we heard he was in a juvenile center and a social worker was involved.

I shouldn't have sent him ahead of me. I could have taken him when I left for the U.S. As I write this story my heart aches, saying to him, "I am so sorry, I am so sorry. I can't even make it up to you." I was able to leave Korea two years later. At that time, he was at a foster home. I got so angry at my sister-in-law for losing the child to Child Protective Services and foster care. After he learned English, he wrote to me, "I want to go home." Why didn't I bring him back home then and he could leave again with me? But we didn't have the money for his travel, nor could I get a visa. So we pleaded with him to put up with a few more months. It was fifty years ago, but it still gives me pain. I cried for this boy then and today.

In those days, my living brother was successful in his construction business and his family was well-off. But I had never asked him for help. My mother, who lived with her wealthy son, had heartache for my Chon Shin Man Ko life (a thousand pains and ten thousand troubles).

But I prayed, "My God, please rescue me from this muddy pit. I would promise you to do anything you want me to do." Was God hearing me? This was my heart-piercing prayer after pushing my son into emotional homelessness in the U.S.

By now, readers might be able to say, Jean Kim lived quite a bit of homeless life in Korea—physically and emotionally. Yes, I sure did. Homelessness can be everyone's experience. I also learned to view homelessness from multiple perspectives: Physical/material, emotional, social and spiritual.

CHAPTER 16

Homelessness
Is Everyone's Story

I have seen it all. I lived through it all. My very own experience allowed me to define the meaning of homelessness from the multidimensional perspectives because I lived them all!

Physical/Material Homelessness

Housing and Urban Development would define it as follows:

An individual who lacks a fixed, regular, and adequate nighttime residence.

An individual who has a primary nighttime residence that is a public or private place not designed for or ordinarily used as a regular sleeping accommodation for human beings, including a car, park, abandoned building, bus or train station, airport, or camping ground.

An individual or family living in a supervised publicly or privately operated shelter designated to provide temporary living arrangements (including hotels and motels paid for by federal, state, or local government programs for low-income individuals or by charitable organizations, congregate shelters, and transitional housing.

An individual who is exiting an institution where he or she temporarily resided and has no place to go.

An individual or family who will imminently lose their housing (as evidenced by a court order they must leave within 14 days).

Emotional Homelessness

I have seen so many people who are so abused, hurt, broken, and deserted by their families, friends and society. When these people lose the meaning and purpose of life, and are being drowned in a "no-good" self-image, hatred, rage, despair, and a destructive lifestyle, they can become emotionally homeless. I have described my own experience of emotional homelessness. I was one who was completely lost, even suffering hallucinations and delusions.

For many, physical homelessness often causes emotional homelessness, and vice versa. They affect one another. Once people fell into physical homelessness their motivation, desire, and hope to live and move forward are all go down the drain. The declaration of trauma informed care and other resources illustrate the impact of emotional homelessness as follows:

1. The event of becoming homeless - of losing one's home, neighbor, routines, accustomed social roles, possible even family members - may itself produce symptoms of psychological trauma in some victims.

2. The ongoing condition of homelessness - living in shelters with such attendant stressors as the possible loss of safety, predictability, and control - may undermine and finally erode coping capabilities and precipitate symptoms of psychological trauma.

3. Becoming homeless and living in shelters may exacerbate symptoms of psychological trauma among people who have histories of victimization."[1]

Someone once said that when the emotional pain is too great to bear, a person's mind goes out of their body into the outer world. That may be called mental illness.

Kierkegaard calls such deep despair "sickness unto death."[2] M.D. May calls this despair "a sin; theologically, sin is what turns us away from love—away from love for ourselves, away from love for one another, and away from love for God. The worst sin is losing hope because it denies God who is the source of hope."[3] I sure have been there!

---

[1] Declaration of Trauma Informed Care: Homelessness as Psychological Trauma: Broadening Perspective, 1991.

[2] Soren Kierkegaard. Sickness unto death (Wilder Publications, 2008), 9.

[3] Gerald G. May, M.D., Addiction and Grace (New York: HarperCollins Publisher, 1988), 2.

Trauma, left untreated, can devastate both the individual and our community: The financial burden to the society of undiagnosed and untreated trauma is staggering. Untreated trauma significantly decreases productivity in the workplace, increases reliance on public welfare, and incarceration rates. The economic costs of untreated trauma-related alcohol and drug abuse alone were estimated at $160.7 billion in 2000.[4]

Social Homelessness

I see many homeless men and women I serve don't have any family members nearby, estranged from them or spouses or grown children, and vice versa. Most of them have no friends they associate with or can count on. I helped nearly forty people get free cell phones from a government program. One condition to get the free phone was presenting a physical address. More than half of them couldn't come up with anyone who could allow them to use their physical home address. No one invites them. They have no place to go. They mostly waste time because no one gives them work. They are nowhere and everywhere on the streets. They seem to be very lonely, isolated, alienated, belong nowhere, and to nobody. They are alone, with no one's care and attention. Some, of course, have drinking or drug problems and abuse and exploit each other. They don't call themselves friends to each other.

A scholarly concept of social isolation refers to a complete or near-complete lack of contact with **people** and **society** for members of a **social species**:

It is usually involuntary, making it distinct from isolating tendencies or actions consciously undertaken by a person, all of which go by various other names. It is also not the same as loneliness rooted in temporary lack of contact with other humans. Social isolation can be an issue for anyone despite their age, each age group may show more symptoms than the other as children are different from adults. Social isolation takes common forms across the spectrum regardless of whether that isolation is self-imposed or is a result of a historical lifelong isolation cycle that has simply never been broken, which also does exist. All types

---

[4] The Economic Costs of Drug Abuse in the United States, 1992-1998.

of social isolation can lead to staying home for days or weeks at a time; having no communication with anyone including family or even the most peripheral of acquaintances or friends; and willfully avoiding any contact with other humans when those opportunities do arise. Even when socially isolated people do go out in public and attempt social interactions, the social interactions that succeed—if any—are brief and at least somewhat superficial. The feelings of loneliness, fear of others, or negative self-esteem can produce potentially very severe psychological injuries. True social isolation over years and decades tends to be a chronic condition affecting all aspects of a person's existence. These people have no one to turn to in personal emergencies, no one to confide in during a crisis, and no one to measure their own behavior against or learn etiquette from—referred to sometimes as social control, but possibly best described as simply being able to see how other people behave and adapt oneself to that behavior. Lack of consistent human contact can also cause conflict with the (peripheral) friends the socially isolated person might occasionally talk to or might cause interaction problems with family members. It may also give rise to uncomfortable thoughts and behaviors within the person.[5]

Some homeless people might have developed social isolation prior to their homeless experience. But many others seemed to fall into social isolation during their homeless life because of being robbed, physically sexually and emotionally abused, used, and exploited, and intentionally they cut off all association with people. They usually superficially related to people at meal programs.

Spiritual Homelessness

I pushed God away with all my might to abandon and nullify my existence. When abused children grow up identifying God with their abusive parents and run away from them and God all together, they can become spiritually homeless. Economic suffering can become the root cause of people's spiritual homelessness when it results in hunger, homelessness, profound hopelessness, and despair that makes them feel

---

[5] From Wikipedia, the free encyclopedia: Social Isolation.

that God has punished and deserted them. Consequently, their lifestyle and behaviors can become destructive to themselves and others and they easily walk away from God and their own life and become spiritually homeless. They might also believe the Church and God side with their oppressors when the Church is denying their access to the house of God just because they are dirty, smelly, disheveled, and at times act strange. Therefore, the behavior of the church can lead the homeless as well as themselves to spiritual homelessness.

My point is that those who consider themselves as devoted Christians with regular spiritual rituals—attending church, bringing offerings, praying, and fasting regularly—can also become spiritually homeless as described in the Scriptures:

> *I hate, I despise your festivals, and I take no delight in your solemn assemblies. Even though you offer me your burnt offerings and grain offerings, I will not accept them; take away from me the noise of your songs; I will not listen to the melody of your harps. But let justice roll down like waters, and righteousness like an ever-flowing stream* (Amos 5: 21-24): *Learn to do good; seek justice, rescue the oppressed, defend the orphan, plead for the widow."* (Isaiah 1:17).

Because we practice all these rituals we think we are acceptable to God, but God doesn't seem to think so.

I remember a story that I heard in Florida:

> One day Jesus was walking down the street. He saw a woman crying outside a church building. He asked, "Why are you crying, sister? She looked up and answered, "Because this church wouldn't let me in as I am a bad-smelling homeless woman." Jesus replied, "Don't worry, sister, they wouldn't let me in either." This story reminds us of Matthew 25:43, 45: Jesus said, *"I was a stranger and you did not welcome me. Just as you did not do it to one of the least of these, you did not do it to me."*

According to this verse the church that didn't welcome her refused Jesus as well and can become spiritually homeless; physically in church but spiritually not in God's heart. My point is that even homed, well-to do ordinary devoted Christians can be spiritually or emotionally homeless, too, depending on what they experience and/or how they relate to God and treat "the oppressed, orphans and widows," who are the homeless people in our day.

In short, anyone can experience physical or emotional, social or spiritual homelessness at one time or another during their lifetime. Therefore, it is not just someone else's experience but can be our own too. All four types of homelessness are all intertwined and affect one another. I had been all of these places: Therefore, it is my own story.

PART SIX

My Calling: Following the Voice

CHAPTER 17

Leaving Thorny Korea

A friend of mine brought me information that the United Church of Christ was accepting applications for volunteers from different parts of the world. So I applied and was accepted. Finally, I was able to leave Korea for good and could see my son.

One process to get a visa was to go through the Korean government's Department of Culture. A supervisor said that cultural exchange wasn't a priority for his recommendations. I challenged him, saying, "I came a long way from Ham Heung, went through *Chon Shin Man Ko*, including the Korean War; now I want to get out to the larger world. Why do you want to keep me in such a small thorny country? Let me go to the larger world and live out my potential." He was shocked to hear that I was from Ham Heung as he, too, came from that town in North Korea. When he heard of my coming from Ham Heung he stamped the paper.

In short, after suffering so much for all my thirty-five years in two Koreas, finally a change had to come! I ran away to the United States, and a year and half later, my husband, Sam, and Sun Kyung (a nanny we adopted) all joined me to pursue a better life in a place where there weren't as many thorns. Thus, the United States became a country of refuge for us.

April 18, 1970, when I was leaving my family and friends behind. Pictured is my family and community, our church family and neighbors who all came to see me off on the day I was leaving Korea.

Yes, God heard my outcry and my prayer! Yes, God opened my prison gate as God opened it for Saint Paul, to get me out of the *Chon Shin Man Ko* muddy pit!

But my heart was broken once again at leaving family behind.

I had been invited to the United States by the Homeland Ministry of the United Church of Christ as one of eleven people from around the world.

I came from a culture that includes the nuclear family, the extended family and the community in our support system. We care for one another. Therefore, I had a difficult time living in a society where only your nuclear family is counted as "family," not even your own parents are included. And it is I- and me-centered and "mine" and "my" success is only counted.

It used to take a month to travel from Korea to the U.S. by boat. But in recent decades it takes half a day by plane. But coming and going wasn't that easy in the sixties and

Members of my immediate and extended family plus a few very close friends.

seventies like it is today. Therefore, going to the U.S. was a big deal for families because they didn't know when they were going to see each

This photo includes our community support system other than family and relatives.

other again. For some older relatives it could have been their last good-bye on earth. Ten people in the photo from my farewell I never saw again. They all passed away.

The Last *Chon Shin Man Ko* Story in Korea

It was a sad day to leave my family behind, but it was also a happy day to be reunited with my son in St. Louis. But I was hit hard by another, last *Chon Shin Man Ko* on Korean soil; suddenly, a few guys showed up at the airport demanding that I pay my husband's debts. This was a total shock, and it was upsetting because I didn't know anything about his debt. They thought that after my departure, it would be impossible to get payment out of him. I was known among his friends as a "certified check." They wanted to take me hostage until the debt was paid. That my husband would go into debt with no plan to pay it back and wouldn't tell me about it since he knew we were barely making it with groceries on credit every month made me so sad that I couldn't stop crying that day.

Tears were running like a broken faucet. It was a heavily taxing day emotionally. Leaving six-year-old Sam, my husband, and my own pain-stricken mother, and all my close relatives and friends was a devastating experience. I cried for several hours without a solution because I didn't have any money. It was not a drama but real life. It was an unbelievable reality for me. When the time to check in approached, finally, my husband's cousin pledged to pay for my husband's debts and I was released. I left for good but with heart-piercing pain for leaving my young boy, Sam, behind. I was so angry that I was swearing that I would never come back. I wanted to leave this *Chon Shin Man Ko* country "for good." So I did!

It had been two years for me to join Hyoung. It was too long of a time for a young boy to be away from his mom and dad. I was foolish for sending him alone.

Having two kids on both sides of the ocean, I was a pain- and tear-stricken woman who cried all the time. I brought it on myself. To find a new life somewhere else, I sacrificed my dear boys. I wasn't a good mother at all. Up to this day, I feel heartache and a huge, never-ending guilt for that.

PART SEVEN

A New Life in the U.S.

CHAPTER 18

Reunion with My Son

As soon as I arrived in St. Louis, before anything else, I went to see Hyoung at the foster care where he was staying. It was a reunion after two years of painful separation. He didn't know what to do with me at first when I suddenly appeared at the house where he was living. That day, we walked all afternoon. Gradually he opened his heart and talked to me and expressed joy.

We walked and walked holding our hands and took many pictures. That day we were the happiest mother and child under the whole sun.

On the other hand, I missed Sam so much that I would hug all the kids I saw that were around his age. I felt a little better since he was with his dad in Korea, but I still missed him so much. Hyoung and I saw each other every day in St. Louis until I left for training, promising him that I would return in a month when the training was over, and that we would live together and never be separated again. So he felt okay about that. I left for Philadelphia for a month of training.

Reunion with my
son Hyoung

Assigned to Camp Moval

When I finished the month-long training, I was assigned to Camp Moval, a retreat center of the Missouri Conference of the United Church of Christ. I was able to take Hyoung with me. He was enrolled in grade school in Union, Missouri, where we lived for one year. On winter nights when no one was around, he taught me how to play the game Yahtzee. I don't know how many hundred games we played. He was telling me all the sad stories he went through while we were separated, which made me cry.

I started to work there in June 1970. My volunteer job for the UCC Homeland Ministry was meeting and speaking to every group that came to Camp Moval for a retreat. During the day, I talked to groups. It was hard to do with my poor English. I used to tell them to ask questions because I didn't know how to start or what to talk about because I had no prior assignments or directions to go on. But when people asked about or commented on the Korean War or the Christian Church, I was excited to speak, especially about the Korean War. The Korean War was my own story, which I lived through and had a lot to say about.

God trained me to speak English here. It was like throwing a non-swimmer into the sea, demanding that he or she swim. My story got around and local UCC churches began to invite me to speak. I ended up speaking to over a hundred different church groups in one year including those that came to the camp for retreat. By the time I finished speaking to a hundred groups, my English got a whole lot better. I became able to speak English. Korean people would say "my mouth opened," which means I became able to speak the language. So this was God's mysterious way of training me.

Ever since, I have been doing public speaking. My friends used to joke, saying, "Even when God calls you back home for good you will say, 'wait God, I must go to speak.'" In fact, I came to the States with a knowledge of English grammar, which helped me learn to speak fast and prevented me from speaking broken English (although English cannot be spoken perfectly unless native born).

From the first day I came to the retreat center, God seemed to watch if I was keeping my promise that "I will do anything you tell me to do." In the evening, I would serve meals and wash dishes in the kitchen and everything and everywhere else where help was needed. I sweated so much that even my underwear were wet. That was not my job, but I worked hard and faithfully in appreciation of living with my son. I used to write monthly report s including the number of groups I spoke to and everything about my activities. My supervisor Rev. Ed Schillingman in Pottstown, Pennsylvania, used to say, "When I read your report I feel like

I'm seeing a movie." He knew every detail of what went on with me there. I was getting room and board and twenty dollars to spend monthly. I had never imagined what he would do for me besides reading my reports. But later he offered a highly commending letter for me to use as my future reference. I had never imagined or had any idea how all these would affect my future life. But I did all the work to keep my pledge with God and to stay faithful.

While I was stationed at the camp, different families invited Hyoung and me to Thanksgiving, Christmas, and other events. We enjoyed very much the first year together this way. Emma Lou, the wife of the camp director, Rev. Ray Bizer, took me to women's meetings and events. We became good friends and attended the church her family attended. Her son and Hyoung also became good friends. Emma Lou and her husband were the first people and mentors in this country whom God prepared to help me out in laying out my foundation in this country nearly fifty years ago. She and her husband now live in New Braunfels, Texas, where her youngest son and his family live nearby. A few years ago, on the way to New Orleans, I stopped by and spent a few days with them. The sad news is that she passed away in April 2018. I lost a chance to see her one more time before she went.

While I was at Camp Moval, the local newspaper carried a story on me. One day, a Korean group showed up at the camp. They were from Gerald, Missouri. Two of them had married GIs. The others were a Korean family. They were so glad to see me, a Korean in that small town. They came every weekend to take me home to Gerald to eat rice and kimchee. We have remained good friends ever since.

The First Sermon

In November of that year, five months after I started to work there, the Good Samaritan Home for the Aged invited me to preach for the Thanksgiving service. How could I do that in my poor English? But I couldn't say no to the request, so I went there with Hyoung. We stayed at Rev. Ebert's house, which was on the compound of the large retirement home. Rev. Ebert was the administrator for the home and his wife was the head nurse there.

Hyoung and I arrived the night before Thanksgiving. It was Wednesday evening when they had a regular weekly social event. I was invited to speak. In my poor English, I shared with them my story, about Korean Christianity, the Korean War, and life at camp, etc. We sang together many songs I liked. They told me that all the songs I liked, popular in Korea at the time, were funeral songs. I had never known that popular hymns the Korean churches were singing were funeral songs. That says a lot about our emotions after going through Chon Shin Man Ko life as a nation.

After the enjoyable evening program singing and talking, we went back to the Eberts' for the night. The next morning, I preached a Thanksgiving service, my first Thanksgiving of 1970 in this country. It was my personal big Thanksgiving God rescuing me from Korea. But how could I thank God for rescuing me while leaving millions of people in Chon Shin Man Ko life back in Korea?

I don't remember everything, but here is part of what I said:

"What is Thanksgiving? Living in the most comfortable and convenient living environment? Eating turkey? At the breakfast table eating eggs with milk sliding down our throat? Comfortably rolling into the sanctuary this morning in wheelchairs? In Korea, in the post-Korean War era, we suddenly ended up having too many homeless children and elderly people who lost their families in the war and were now living a poverty-stricken life. What will be their Thanksgiving be today? Would they thank God for being alive after losing their beloved children and spouse? They can't even imagine the kind of life you are enjoying over here. What is our Thanksgiving this morning?"

After Thanksgiving Service, Rev. Ebert suggested that I work for him after finishing my volunteer work at the camp. At least that's what I thought he said because sometimes his English wasn't clear, and he mumbled a lot. I replied, "I don't know." He suggested that I think it over when I get back to the camp. I told my supervisor, Rev. Bizer, about the offer and he encouraged me to take it. So I called Rev. Ebert to accept his job offer when my time at the camp was over.

CHAPTER 19

Blessed New Life

When I finished my one-year service in May 1971, I slid in to the Good Samaritan Home for the Aged with my boy. It was a beautiful setting built on the bank of Mississippi River. My job was assistant social worker. The job came with a two-bedroom apartment, adjacent to the retirement home, with a small pay of $200 a month and two meals a day. Hyoung and I walked to the grocery store and came back by taxi. It was too far to walk with groceries in hand.

A Blessed Job

The job and housing were blessings that simply fell on my lap from heaven. It was as if God had prepared it for me. Otherwise, nothing like this could have happened. This means ever since I ran to the U.S. I had never looked for a job or housing. It was all God's doing, therefore, it was God's story. All of it, from the first day up to this point, it was God's story. No other way or any human vocabulary can explain.

My job was working in the infirmary, on the sixth floor, doing recreational therapy, which I had never done before. The rest of the five floors were filled with rather healthy retirees. I had to create activities for the elderly, who were bed and/or chair-bound. I got them up in wheelchairs, encouraged them to sing their old songs, make some ornaments, play their familiar games. I myself learned a lot from that experience and often I listened to their old stories and did some counseling too. I was a very cheerful, grateful, and encouraging friend. I was well accepted and welcomed into their lives. They called all this "recreational therapy." I had to create something from nothing, not from experience but with a brand-new start.

I performed the job well, learning from volunteers and the head social worker. Most of the elderly there had highly respectful professions in their early life. But now they were aged, their bodies fading away from illness, and the only thing left for them was loneliness. I respected where they came from and who they were today, and I tried to use their remaining potential and possibilities that were yet lingering in them. Emotionally, they were homeless, if you will. What I could do was careful and friendly listening, loving them, and creating and doing fun projects with them.

I thanked God for discipling me with the English language and teaching me to share my time and talent with others at the camp. And then, God also trained and disciplined me to love people who were living their physically hopeless last stage of life at the Good Samaritan Home. God's careful and tedious training and discipline amazes me again and again. I thank God for such discipline.

This job was an impossible one for a non-citizen alien to even dream about. But they considered my social work experience in Korea and recommendation from Rev. Ed Shillingman and Rev. Ray Bizer of the camp very highly. They also considered the fact that the life of the bed-ridden elderly began to brighten with my presence. My one-year volunteer work from the bottom up helped lay a foundation down one brick at a time, which I had never realized at the time, but did simply to my pledge to God.

We went to Trinity UCC Sunday mornings, which was in South St. Louis. Hyoung and I walked a mile to the church. We went to a Korean Church in the afternoon in Clayton, Missouri, which was fifteen miles away. Some people picked us up and brought us back.

In those crowded cars, I felt a strong need to have our own vehicle. While we were walking to grocery stores, Hyoung and I pointed at all the cars saying, "I want this car. I want that car." I studied the driver guidebook and passed the written test with a perfect score. I then hired a driving teacher from a driving school. It cost one hundred dollars for five lessons. When I was receiving driving lessons, Hyoung sat in the back seat and watched me. A week later, I passed the driving test and got a license.

I needed to save money to buy a used car. Since I was only earning small amounts of cash in addition to two meals a day and a free apartment, it was hard to save much. So this is what I did: In those days, they sold packages of chicken bones and necks for fifteen cents. I bought it for myself and bought meat for Hyoung. I was already saving a bit, and eventually, I came up with six hundred dollars.

One day I asked a friend of mine in the insurance business to find a used car for me. He and his wife used to invite Hyoung and I to dinner during holidays such as Thanksgiving. For my six hundred dollars, the insurance man brought me an old used white Ford four-door sedan, including insurance coverage. Since I knew nothing about cars, he chose it for me. So I began to drive that car. I did practice driving on the highway every Sunday morning when fewer cars were on the road. Hyoung and I went to the grocery store, to Union to visit the Bizers and went to see my sister-in-law and the Korean Church in Clayton. Hyoung and I sat in the car and scrubbed and cleaned it so often that people used to say, "You are going to wear out the car by washing and scrubbing it." We loved this old car, our first one!

Reunion with My Family

A year and a half later since Hyoung and I settled in our apartment at the Good Samaritan Home, my husband came with Yong Soo (Sam) and Sung Kyung, our adopted daughter, who was older than Hyoung.

Good Samaritan Home gave my husband a job in the infirmary as a physical therapist when the administrator and a nurse (his wife) heard that my husband was a sportsman. In fact, my employer promised to hire my husband way before he came. I told him not to do that until he met my husband. But he said he felt safe to give him a job knowing who I was and how I was doing.  I told him my husband was not like me at all, but my employer didn't listen. So my husband had to start work the day after his arrival. He lucked out since many newcomers with poor English used to find it hard to find a job, even a labor job. But he got a physical therapist's job in an infirmary! Since he, too, got lunch and housing, his pay was low, but we appreciated it so much. It was God's package blessing. He had never looked for a job in this country. Again, it was absolutely God's story.

The latecomers—Sung Kyung and Sam—both enrolled in Mann's Grade School in our neighborhood. The children there were all white. They didn't seem to understand kids from another culture. My children were beaten up a lot. I taught them to walk away from bully kids. Hyoung once challenged me, asking, "Should I walk away even when kids beat me up?"

One day he came home bleeding from his legs. Perhaps kids threw rocks at him. I was deeply disturbed and went to see their parents. There was no parent. Another time, another kid beat up my children. I visited this child's home. I met his father who served in Korea and said he knew Korean children were well-disciplined, but U.S. children are not. He apologized, pledging to teach his child better. Our kids were teased as "Jap," "nigger," "Chinaman."

Eventually, I called the school principal and reported to him that the children calling my children all kinds of racial slurs and asked if his school could help students to understand culturally different people. He said, the school couldn't do anything because the discrimination came from their parents. I told him that if the school wouldn't help, I was going to teach my children to defend themselves. I warned him that if anything happened, it wasn't my responsibility. Discrimination could come from parents, but the school should try to help students. I began to tell my boys to defend themselves, by sending them to karate school. I drove my boys ten miles to their martial arts school every afternoon after their regular school.

One summer day when my two boys were making too much noise in the apartment, which was right next door to a resident's apartment, I sent both boys to the post office to mail letters and buy some stamps. As they came out of the post office with some change in Hyoung's pocket, suddenly a bigger guy appeared behind Hyoung and grabbed his neck and began choking him, demanding the money. Out of desperation, Sam picked up a rock, saying, "If you don't let go of my brother, I'm going to throw this rock at you." The would-be robber let Hyoung go.

My husband didn't get along with the nurses, who told him what to do. He quit his job and moved out, while I stayed. He opened a wig store with help from his sister, who knew something about them, although it was the first time my husband ever even touched one.

From American Dream to the Jesus Dream

When I got here everything was beautiful, abundant, and comfortable. It was an entirely different world. There was the promise of the American Dream for any person if he or she wanted it. However, to my surprise, my desire to pursue the American dream gradually faded away from me. Because I feared that following the American dream would distance me farther and farther away from Jesus, who was born, lived, loved, served, and died homeless and left his legacy for us to follow. I did not want to forget or let go of this image of Jesus that had inspired me profoundly ever since my teen years. Therefore, the pursuit of the American Dream made me feel as if I were betraying Jesus. Not so much to pursue the American Dream, but rather to survive, my husband engaged in a small business. Whenever I stepped in to help, the sales went up. If I partnered in the business, we could have achieved the American Dream faster. But then I remembered my fear that making lots of money could take me away from the Jesus dream. Back then, like everyone around me, I was equating the American Dream with wealth.

What is the American Dream Anyway?

According to scholars, the term "American Dream" first was used by the American writer and popular historian James Truslow Adams (1878–1949) in his 1931 book *The Epic of America*. At that time, the United States was suffering under the Great Depression. Adams used the term to describe the complex beliefs, religious promises and political and social expectations. He stated that the American Dream was "that dream of a land in which life should be better and richer and fuller for everyone, with opportunity for each according to ability or achievement."[6] Originally, the idea of the American Dream is rooted in the United States Declaration of Independence.[7]

[6] James Truslow Adams. *The Epic of America* (New York: Blue Ribbon Books, 1931). 214-215.
[7] James Truslow Adams. *The Epic of America* (New York: Blue Ribbon Books, 1931). 214-215.

However, John E. Nestler reflects in an essay, *Whereas the American Dream*, as once equated with certain principles of freedom, it is now equated with things. The American Dream has undergone a metamorphosis from principles to materialism. . . . When people are concerned more with the attainment of things than with the maintenance of principles, it is a sign of moral decay. And it is through such decay that loss of freedom occurs."[8]

What Is the Jesus Dream Then?

For me, he came to the lowliest places like the poor/homeless, lived homeless, served and loved the most poor/sick/abandoned homeless as a homeless person himself by entirely emptying all of himself, and died the loneliest death of the homeless (although God raised and vindicated him). I see my homeless friends in the homeless life and death of Jesus; one who died an unfair and premature death on the cross. John Shelby Spong helps me to express much better who Jesus was:

When his disciples forsook him, he loved his forsakers. When one of them denied him and another betrayed him, he loved the denier and the betrayer. When his enemies abused him, he loved his abusers. When they killed him, he loved his killers. He was the one condemned to die, but he gave his life away even as they took it from him. He gave forgiveness to the soldiers (Luke 23:34). He gave assurance to the penitent thief (Luke 23:43). Here was a whole human being who lived fully, who loved wastefully, and who had the courage to be himself under every set of circumstances. He was thus a human portrait of the meaning of God, understood as the source of life, the source of love, and the ground of being.[9]

For me, learning the footsteps of this Jesus is following the Jesus Dream. The American Dream would have kept me away from this image of complete love, and sacrificial sharing.

---

[8]John E. Nestler. *The American Dream.* Published, October 1973 issue of The Freeman, John E. Nestler

[9]John Shelby Spong, *Why Christianity Must Change or Die* (San Francisco: HarperSanFrancisco, 1998), 128.

A Heavenly Gift of a Home

Our kids began to annoy the elderly at the retirement home with their loud play, so we decided to move out. But no one would rent an apartment to us because we were too large a family with three kids. We began to look at old houses just for fun with no possibility to rent or buy since we didn't have a penny in our hands. One day we looked at a five-bedroom old mansion house, but with no possibility to do anything with it. The owner got us a realtor but what can he do for a family of five with no money? Then the owner got a new job, and needed to sell his house quickly. He made an impossible deal with the realtor. The owner will put down-payment for us which the realtor was supposed to add to our home loan while we just make the monthly mortgage payment. Including an attic and a basement, where the boiler and laundry machine were, it was a four-story house. The price of this sixty-year-old house was $2,000 in 1974. The owner couldn't take everything with him since he was downsizing, so left almost all of his furniture for us. Without a penny, we ended up with a furnished house.

The day we moved in, Sam sat on the stairs and shouted, "This is mine! This is mine!" There is no other vocabulary for such a miraculous happening except "the heavenly gift of a home." Again, God opened heaven's gate and showered such unexpected blessings upon us.

Other Korean church friends around us didn't

The first house we bought in St. Louis.

believe our story. They kept asking, where did you get the money? You have been in this country only for a few years and bought a mansion? Where did the funds came from? Some of them were even suspicious of us. Our answer was "it was God's gift."

CHAPTER 20

Birth of the Democracy Movement in Korea

It was the mid 1970s when Korea was being living under president Park Chung Hee's authoritarian rule. Kim Dae Jung was accused of being a communist sympathizer and severely persecuted as a result. In Korea at the time, not too many people could stand up protesting against such unfair accusations from fear of being arrested. So Christian scholars in the U.S. and Canada joined together to raise their voices and to develop the "Save Kim Dae Jung" movement. Since we lived in St. Louis, we hosted meetings several times. Dr. Jai Joon Kim was our most respected scholar, who taught us at the Han Shin Seminary along with Rev. Stephen Moon and Professor Oo Jung Lee. However, at one of the conferences held in St. Louis this group split over ideological differences. Dr. Sun woo Hakwon represented the group, claiming, "unification first," which meant it didn't matter to him whether the unification came with communist

or democratic ideology. Dr. Jai Joon Kim represented "democracy first." We went with this ideology because we didn't want to live under communist rule. Since we were blessed with a huge home, we once hosted ten meeting participants, all prominent leaders of Korea, who were then residing in

the U.S. or Canada. This was the first democracy movement in Korea while we lived in the U.S.

I can never forget Rev. Dr. Jai Joon Kim. The reason why we participated in Korean Democracy movement in the U.S. was the late Dae Jung Kim (the former President of Korea) and the late Dr. Jai Joon Kim. Both of them were heavily involved in the movement in the dark era of the seventies and eighties, when the Korean authoritarian regime didn't mind arresting many people, and torturing and even killing them. Once Doo Hwan Chun (one of the former presidents) massacred almost the whole town of Kwang Ju. While we were living in

St. Louis, the big shots such as Jai Joon Kim, Sang Don Kim (the former mayor of Seoul), and Rev. Jai Rin Moon stayed at our big house as they participated in our annual events.

More Education

Clinical Pastoral Education

By this time, I got to know many leaders in the United Church of Christ system. Once they asked me if I wanted to be ordained, but I said no. I had never thought about it. Had I been motivated then, I could have had a wonderful opportunity to study at Eden Seminary on full scholarship, under wonderful scholars. I guess I wasn't ready for it then. But I was interested in Clinical Pastoral Education. That was a one-year program held at the UCC-affiliated Deaconess Hospital. It was a wonderful eye-opening learning experience. We even observed surgery and an autopsy.

Master's Degree in Social Work (1975–1977)

The Good Samaritan Home loved me and was good to me. However, at one point, a student who was doing an internship under me was earning more than I was. I got angry because I took it as racial discrimination. What was I to do with my emotion? Should I complain about it as an alien? Who would hear me out? I didn't do anything, lest I leave a bad record behind me. Instead, I went to St. Louis University and registered for a master's in social work program, which I paid for with a student loan. I quit my assistant social work job and helped my husband's business while studying.

Because I wasn't sure if my English was good enough to do master's level study, I asked Korean students in the program which class was the most difficult. They all said it was the human behavior course, so I started with that to test my qualification. It was a very interesting class, but the teacher was tough and made us read seventy-eight articles in one semester. My reading was slow and I had a heck of a time reading all of those materials and taking three two-hour tests during the semester. But I made it and I qualified myself. The next semester I took two courses. I passed those too. The second year I registered as a full-time student, finishing the whole program in three years. I did a one-year practicum at Wohl Memorial Mental Hospital, which was part of St. Louis University Medical School's Department of Psychiatry. In May 1977, I received my degree focusing on mental health. Ever since I dropped out of the University of Chicago in 1960, I always kept the dream to go back someday and finish my degree. And seventeen years later, at age forty-two, I sure did finish it, although the degree wasn't theology this time. Nonetheless, what a good feeling to achieve something like this. I'm so glad that I went back to college at such a late date. Thank God for that! My kids supported my study. Hyoung used to meet me at the bus stop when I would come home late, walking with me on the dangerous dark street and asking if I did okay on my tests. He was only fourteen but already a young man who protected his mother.

Well-Paid Full-Time Job

Right after I got my MSW degree, my first job was to work for the St. Clair County Community Mental Health Center, located in East St. Louis, Illinois, as a day-treatment coordinator for the mentally ill and developmentally disabled. Fifty percent of those who participated in the

day-treatment program were developmentally disabled and the other half were mentally ill. I had eleven staff under me, most of whom were people of color. We had one bus that transported patients to and from the center.

Some lived in shelters and others in their low-income housing with parents or someone else, and some lived on the street.

The job was too big for a brand-new social worker, but somehow the position fell on me. It was entirely by the grace of God. I drove fifteen miles every morning from South St. Louis, Missouri, crossing a bridge to East St. Louis, Illinois. While I was there, I wrote for a grant that helped us fill our storage with educational materials and non-perishable food. I even offered staff an in-service by inviting faculty members from Southern Illinois University. I renovated an old huge office space for eleven staff, taking partitions out and scrubbing an old stove to make it look like a shiny new one. We cooked hot lunches every day for day-treatment participants. It was a huge job. I was either naive or fearless. God threw me again into this unknown river for me to swim and survive.

Meeting mentally ill substance-addicted people in poverty-stricken East St. Louis was a new experience. I did active outreach with them wherever they were in the community. East St. Louis was a predominantly African American community I wasn't familiar with at all culturally. Again, I jumped into it, thinking we are all the same human beings created and called as God's children. After all, they were all lovable people. I ended up closely and deeply bonded with them. Dr. Amanda Murphy, the top administrator in psychology, herself an African American, married to a white medical doctor, ended up calling me "an angel sent from heaven." Wow! Did I deserve this? No way!

CHAPTER 22

So Proud of My Two Sons

Everything was going well, busy life running a hundred miles an hour, with the rewarding feeling of having my family together and watching the boys grow up. Hyoung was getting his first prize academic award from Man's Junior High—the first time a minority boy called "Jap," "nigger," and "Chinaman" got the first prize in the whole graduating class. The all-white-school hated this and applied the SAT twice hoping that one of their white boys would get it. But Hyoung, my dear son, kept getting the first prize with his tests. Finally, the school had to offer him the first prize with a nickname "the most talented" or "walking encyclopedia."

Sam's confirmation when he was 15 at the Trinity United Church of Christ in St. Louis, Missouri.

Hyoung getting the honor of first prize from Jr. High graduating class with the title of most talented or "walking encyclopedia."

Sam and Hyoung with trophies

My two boys got so many trophies.

PART EIGHT

Despair:
Sickness Unto Death

My World Collapses

When I came to the United States, I lost my native country, home, culture, mother, eldest brother, close friends, and many of my very intimate relatives. Despite leaving so much behind, my husband and I and our two sons and daughter were hopeful and happy to build our life anew in the U.S.

For the first seven years, we were working so hard to survive that we didn't realize when the flowery spring had come and gone. The seven years had gone by like seven months.

In the eighth year of our immigration, in 1978, a devastating trauma hit me hard. I was knocked down and fell into a deep, dark ditch of hopelessness when I had to face the sudden death of my seventeen-year-old son, Hyoung. Don't ask me why and where? Up to this day, it is too painful to talk about it.

It has been exactly forty years ago that this happened. It has been too painful to talk or write about how and what happened. Crying and grieving for forty years! Are there any more tears left in my eyes? Yes, plenty of them are still there!

It was like being bombed or stepping on a mine and being blown into a thousand pieces. On that day, the sun and the moon seemed to disappear from my life. I hit the lowest point of my life in heart-piercing pain and anguish as heavy in guilt as if the weight of heaven and earth had collapsed on my chest. Of all my losses—my mother, eldest brother, my second nephew—the loss of a child was the most devastating. My pain was like a bombshell struck and stuck in my heart ever since and never went away. I woke up weeping, cooked weeping, ate weeping, went to work weeping, went to bed weeping, worshipped weeping and sang weeping. I was hallucinating; sensing some invisible movement moving along with me whenever I was moving around in the house. I was hearing movements and sound out of the closet from my son's room. I even re-experienced the pain of childbirth for one whole year. I was delusional that some men in black suits were hiding behind every door in the house. I felt someone's presence behind me all the time. I was so scared that I had to sit leaning on the wall so that nothing was behind me. All this led me to active suicidal ideation; I didn't want to live anymore. I had had enough pain and anguish in my life. I argued with God, *"This is IT! I can't take*

anymore pain. My life must end here. Take it. Cancel my existence and blot me out of this world. Let the earth open its mouth to swallow me. Don't love me, forgive me, feel sorry for me, comfort me, or save me. I don't want to live any longer in this world. I am not worthy as a woman, as a mother, or even as a human being after burying my dear child in the ground. Please kill me, take me away, O God. It was all my fault."

Kierkegaard named such a profound despair "sickness unto death." Yes, I was sick unto death! I was emotionally and spiritually lost, homeless, walking around like a zombie. But even in such despair, I went to work and performed my job and daily activities as usual.

But I kept pushing God away from me with all my strength. The Bible says Jacob wouldn't let God go, wrestling with God all night to be blessed, but I wrestled with God for 365 nights, a whole year to let God go from me and I wanted to be condemned to death.

I Pushed God Away

God grabbed me tight, wouldn't let me go and argued with me by saying, *"You are denying me because love, compassion, mercy, hope and forgiveness are the very essence of me. If you deny accepting these, you deny my existence."* I argued back, "No, that's not true. If I hadn't recognized your being, how could I have requested you do these things for me?" I kept wrestling with God, pushing him away from me with all my strength. But I could not kill myself because I knew that I didn't own my life, God did. I wanted to lose myself just like the mentally disturbed patients I was working with, but it wasn't happening, although some of my friends thought I was losing myself.

Jesus's Weeping Touch

One late afternoon I was crying my heart out at my son's grave site. I sensed someone touching my shoulder. I lifted my tear-stained face and saw a gentleman sitting next to me. His face, too, was covered with his tears. He asked me why I was crying like that and I answered that I had buried my child there. I asked him why he was crying. He said his father was buried right next to my son. He then asked if I had a church.

"Yes, I go to an English speaking and Korean speaking church," I told him.

He asked again, "Then, how come you are alone like this?"

I told him, "Today I feel all alone under the sun."

That afternoon, his tears appeared to be Jesus's tears as if he was crying with me. And his touching hand on my shoulder felt like Jesus's warm hands.

Ever since this experience, it became my confession that I had seen the weeping Jesus and experienced Jesus's touch. Truly, I felt that Jesus was crying with me. Yes, I felt his heart ache whenever my heart was broken and pierced.

Surrender

All along, God didn't want to hear me out and do what I was requesting. Rather, God confronted me with a message, "You are denying my existence by your insensible request. This challenging message awakened my soul to the fact that what I was asking God to do was an unrealistic request that can never be performed for anyone. In the end, God's steadfastness and perseverance won the fight over me. I finally surrendered allowing *"God to do anything with me because this life of mine I didn't want and even dogs wouldn't eat it."* Ever since, God has been dictating my life and I haven't have anything to do except for my absolute obedience as an absolute loser. God possessed and enslaved me. If God says "go," I go. If God says "do," I do. Therefore, I no longer existed but only for God. If I lived, I lived for God. If I must die, I would die for God. I didn't know what else I could do as an absolute loser.

CHAPTER 24

Leaving the Dead City

St. Louis, welcoming me and my family, was once my second hometown. I made so many friends and settled down so well that I felt at home there, and thus there was no other place I should live under the sun. But now it was the dead city. There was no joy as a home like there used to be. In an absolute dark despair, I cried all the time. When I passed the park where my kids used to play, I cried; when I passed their school area, I cried; when I passed the hamburger shop we used to eat at together, I cried; when I passed the church we attended together, I cried; when I passed stores where we shopped together, I cried. In my waking hours and in my sleep, I cried, except when I was performing my job at work. For the whole year I wandered between home, work, and his grave. My husband finally suggested we move to Seattle where he knew someone. He couldn't stand my weeping anymore.

A Vision

The night before our departure from St. Louis—the dead city—for Seattle, I had a dream: A tall tree with full branches was set on fire. This burning tree looked exactly like the one behind my son's gravesite. Next minute, the tree turned into ashes and then out of the ashes flowers were blooming—fire to ashes to flowers! It was awesome and mysterious. All the way to Seattle, I kept questioning my husband about what the house he bought for us looked like, asking, "Does that house have a large living room?" In the back of my head, I had a vision of starting a church in our living room. But I didn't say anything to him about this mysterious thought and I kept it to myself.

It took a whole week from St. Louis to Seattle by car because we could drive only during the day. That was the year we had a gas crisis. All filling stations would close from dusk until dawn. While driving out to Seattle, the whole week we both cried on and off in our car, asking ourselves where we were going and why.

PART NINE

Another New Life

CHAPTER

25

Moving to Seattle

In July of 1979, we moved into our new home in Seattle, Washington. My husband went ahead of me to find a new house, and after finding one, came back to St. Louis to get me. After our arrival in Seattle, my visions to do a church faded away. We were very busy setting up our small business to survive. In this new environment all my hallucinations were also completely gone, although I kept weeping as much as ever.

Our new house in Seattle, Washington

Power of the Holy Spirit

However, something was forcing me to read the Bible day and night. I had never read the Bible that much in my entire life: I read the whole Good News Bible, the whole Living Bible, the whole Revised Standard Bible, the whole International Version Bible, and the whole New Revised Standard Bible plus a few Korean versions. I ended up exclaiming, "Now I see the light. I see the light, and my eyes are open!" In the past I couldn't see anything except darkness—no hope except despair. A few years had gone by without anything else happening after that awesome dream I had in St Louis. Quite often God spoke to me this way through visions, but I did not understand what the message was! It took much longer to understand the meaning of the visions.

CHAPTER 26

Democracy Movement
and Persecution

I t was May of 1980 when many young people in Kwang Ju, Korea,
took to the streets to protest the dictatorship of Chun Doo Hwan,
then president. He sent paratroops to Kwang Ju to mercilessly butcher
demonstrators. The dead kids in the photos looked just like my own
deceased son. My husband and I were so devastated that we organized
the Korean-American Human Rights Council to support and stand in
solidarity with the grieving people of Kwangju for the loss of their precious
children. We also planned a memorial service for the victims. Although
as theology graduates, my husband and I could officiate the service, we
invited Seattle-area Korean pastors to lead the service. None of them
showed up. Probably they were fearful of being accused as communist
sympathizers. Kwangju victims
were so condemned by the
Korean president and his
administration. So my husband
and I led the memorial service.

Of course, our efforts to
support the struggle of the
Kwangju people brought us
harsh accusations that we were
communist sympathizers, and
we were harassed by Korean

Rev. Jack Wilson is speaking against
merciless massacre.

immigrants who were blindly supporting the Korean government. We
ended up losing everything through bankruptcy, including our home and

small business. The small business my husband had set up was an Asian grocery store for which most customers were Korean Americans. They stopped shopping at our store lest they, too, be accused as communist sympathizers. Some even spread a rumor that we were "communist." To make things worse, there was another competing Asian grocery story that

was started by another Korean American near our store. There was a rumor that the Korean consulate office in Seattle planted one to compete with ours and defeat us.

Protesting the human rights violations of the Korean government in the early 1980s

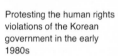

We invited Kim, Dae Jung, (before he became the president of Korea) to Seattle as a speaker. Kane Hall of the University of Washington was packed. Although people were scared to participate in our street protest, they came to hear him.

Human Rights Award

Our own natives were condemning us based on unfounded accusations. But the Seattle Chapter of the United Nations Association gave me a human rights award in 1981, the first of twenty-four awards I received, though the others were mostly for community service.

CHAPTER 27

Ordination:
Path Toward Ministry

At first, I wasn't ready. I thought social work was my ministry. But then, maybe that was not what God planned for me.

I experienced hitting rock bottom several times in my life; I had come through refugee life, the Korean War, losing a brother, falling from wealth to poverty, homelessness, and losing a child. When I lost my son, I thought that was it. I've already mentioned that I had demanded that God take my life away, but ended up surrendering to God and allowing him to do anything he wanted to do with my life. With this surrender, God opened a whole new world for me to work with purple people—the homeless population. I used to demand that God send my son back. Now when I look back, I remember a message from God that was, "*I cannot give your son back, but I give you many, many lost lives.*" I remember responding, "When did I say I want many of those lives? I just want my son back."

Somehow, I sensed a mysteriously notion of ordination secretly creeping into my heart. Up until then, I had never dreamed of being ordained. In the past, there were several opportunities to become ordained in St. Louis, but I had no interest in it at all. But this time, I let Rev. Jack Wilson, then pastor of my church (Maplewood Presbyterian) know about  this. He supported my mysterious vision wholeheartedly. Before I knew it, the ordination process had already begun. He then had the church session take me under its care and began to work with the Committee on Ministry of the North Puget Sound Presbytery.

On the day in 1986 that the North Puget Sound Presbytery took me in as an inquirer, my confession to the whole presbytery in ever-flowing tears was that, *"If I live, I live for the Lord, and if I die, I die for the Lord; whether I live or die, I am the Lord's, for Christ lifted up the corpse of Jean Kim and breathed life into it. I had already gone through and lost a lot, and nothing seemed to be left for me anymore except to serve the Lord and die for my Lord Jesus."* It was so true that there was nothing left for me in this world except doing what God told me to do. People later told me that there wasn't dry eye in the presbytery gathering that day.

God picked up this garbage that had been thrown away and made it useful for God's mission. God put some light into my soul and I ended up exclaiming, "Now I see the light! I see the light!" God planted a renewed motivation in my soul to serve the Lord again. I undertook more schooling at the Seattle chapter of Fuller Seminary while working a full-time job at Harborview Community Mental Health Center in Seattle. It was a spiritually joyful experience, but also a challengingly heavy burden and physically unbearable.

More Theological Education and Ordination

My experience at Fuller Seminary was a good one, gaining additional sources of theological knowledge such as the New Testament Theology, the Old Testament Theology, Exegesis, Homiletics, the Church History,

etc. The seminary also took many years of my social service as elective credits. After passing the written ordination exam that came down from the General Assembly, and the preliminary and final oral examination by the North Puget Sound Presbytery (now

Northwest Coast Presbytery), ordination became an unbelievable reality for me at age fifty-two (April 12, 1987). The ceremony was bilingual: the sermon, prayer, charge, and choir were all in English and Korean. The food was also American and Korean. Could this be the answer to the vision of ashes turned into blooms? Some of my friends interpreted the dream as a resurrection from my own death.

After the ordination, I experienced absolute peace of mind as if I was on morphine. I had never experienced such a perfect and absolute peaceful state of mind before or after this event. It could have been the outcome of complete laying-down or emptying all of myself to let only Jesus Christ live in me. It was just a pure gift from God.

Campus Christian Ministry

In the Presbyterian Church system, you must have a call to be ordained. My call came from Ecumenical Campus Christian Ministry at the University of Washington, Seattle, to develop a ministry for international students. Again, the Holy Spirit carried me for seven years on her wing: I had to develop something that hasn't existed before. So, I began to do active outreach to students at their departments, lunchrooms, activities, and their residence. Every fall, I offered a welcome party for new international students.

With good barbecue food in the yard of Covenant House, we usually had a lively full house for the welcome party. My mission was integrating faith, worship, Bible study, prayers and politics  since it was an era when many third-world countries experienced dictatorial rules imprisoning prominent opposing voices. In South Korea, Kim Dae Jung was imprisoned. In South Africa, Mandela was imprisoned. In the Philippines, Marcos put opposing voices in prison. In Burma, Aung San Suu Kyi was imprisoned. However, the U.S. faith communities wanted

to hide behind their complacent spirituality. I used to invite the Seattle-area ecumenical church community and the University of Washington political science faculties or PhD candidates from the third world to speak to us on the role of the United States and its faith communities in such a world political climate. We learned from the Korean situation that voices coming from the U.S. faith communities were very encouraging and supportive to those struggling with their fight for peace and justice out of prison. People from the wider community, including the university, community responded very positively. We then enjoyed an Asian dinner together. It became an opportunity to integrate our Christian faith and our responsibility for society and the world. When I was retiring, one of my colleagues commented that an era was over.

In June 1989, Sam Graduated from U.W.

PART TEN

Marching Purple People

CHAPTER 28

Marching Purple Women

Everyone's life might be difficult. But to me, my life appeared to be a harder one. However, it was not all bad all the time. There were times when light was shining in with good things happening. In fact, I was able to develop quite a few missions during my *Chon Shin Man Ko* life. That by itself would occupy the space of an entire volume. Therefore, here I am going to share some significant ones under the title of "Marching Purple People" because my purple friends don't have to suffer all the time either. They can march toward a better future. Our homeless women used to sing with their whole hearts, "When the Saints go marching in . . . I want to be in that number." And we repeated, "Marching, marching, we are marching."

A Vision

While I was working at Harborview Community Mental Health Center as a mental health practitioner before I was ordained, I met many patients who came into the mental health ward after attempting suicide. I thought to myself, "Had God been in their life, they might not have attempted to take their own lives." And later, when I was assigned as a mental health practitioner to three women's shelters (Angeline, YWCA downtown, and Lutheran Compass Center), I met many emotionally troubled homeless women there too. Then I realized that their spiritual needs couldn't be met by good mental health treatment/counseling and good case management services alone. I began to conceive of a vague notion that with my background (theology, social work, and mental health), I might have something to offer. But I didn't do anything about it at the time.

Years later, however, when I rediscovered that there were too many homeless women in downtown Seattle, it troubled me, and I couldn't be complacent any longer.

I have had several visions of God's calling toward this. I was working in two half-time jobs; one serving Christian campus ministry at the University of Washington and the other working at the Harborview Community Mental Health Center in downtown Seattle. It was exactly a year after my ordination, April 3, 1988, Easter morning when I had a dream that I was standing inside the front door of a small one-room church. Out of a huge unburning fire, God was speaking to me to *"plant a cross right where you are standing; it will grow through the roof."* It was so crystal clear and awesome that I was deeply moved and trembled, and I will remember it vividly forever.

In response to the dream, although not fully understanding the meaning of it, I added more spiritual programs at Campus Ministry. I didn't know

how else to respond. But I kept that dream deep in my heart and kept wondering what God could have been saying to me?

One day I was admitted to Stevens Hospital with dangerously high blood pressure and severe chest pain. In the hospital bed, I mumbled to God that I didn't have time to lie in a hospital bed, and what exactly was the meaning of "planting a cross"? In a dozing state, the whole room turned snow white and the meaning of the dream became crystal clear: I must do ministry with the homeless women. I thought to myself, had God taken my life last night, what good would it have been to have a well-paying job with good benefits. Then I responded to God once again saying, *"Yes, yes, I will do it."* I thanked God for clarifying the meaning of the awesome vision.

This vision meant that God picked me up from the ashes and revived me to full life. Because when I lost my child, I pushed God away, refusing to be comforted only demanding to be let go, abandoned and my existence nullified. Therefore, this was a moment that I was welcoming God back into my life.

Church of Mary Magdalene/Mary's Place

After I came home from the hospital I began to worship with five homeless women whom I had known from the mental health system. Thus, the church of Mary Magdalene was born in Seattle on January 19, 1991, with these five women, serving them on weekends because I was still working full time. Word got out. In no time, the number of worshippers grew.

Later as I understood, "**planting a cross**" meant not the dead wooden cross but *"planting the living cross that represents all who Jesus is, his absolute love, care, compassion, forgiveness, sacrifice, emptying, sharing, and hope for the despaired homeless, and excluded ones."* So, my mission was planting the cross in the souls of my homeless friends and supporters as well.

Some women had just started living on the street. But I had one woman who had been on the street for sixteen years. A year ago, I got her an apartment. Some had just been evicted or were running from abusive husbands or paranoia. In both their early and adult lives, many women had been abused and damaged physically, emotionally, and spiritually by their parents or parental figures, or spouses and partners, often in the name of God. In their homeless lives they continued to be abused, robbed, or raped and even murdered; their lives were overcome with threats and fear. What had resulted from such experiences was a low and negative self-image, and despair that led to destructive behavior to self, others, and society. Many of them were fearful to be around men and some were even paranoid. Therefore, I was motivated to create a worshipping environment for homeless women alone that was safe, accepting, caring, loving, sharing, and supporting. Thus, I developed this church for homeless women to be inclusive, holistic, touching every aspect of women's lives. Thus, God, homeless women, and the whole community could march together to restore women's pride, self-image, and dignity.

1. **The purpose** of this church as drawn from John 20:8 where Mary Magdalene exclaimed, *"I have seen the Lord,"* with the hope that homeless women may repeat her announcement by coming into the presence of Jesus Christ, who welcomed many broken women in his time and healed them. As Mary Magdalene rose, they, too, might rise from their past wounds, homelessness, despair and hopelessness by restoring their broken relationship with God, themselves, others and society so that they join the march of Mary Magdalene.

2. The purpose was based in the belief that God created women and men in God's own image and blessed them equally to enjoy the abundance on the earth (Gen. 1:26-28), plus have a home to live in. By restoring the lost pride, self-worth, and the image that God created originally, women would feel better about themselves, and would be motivated to get up, walk, and be productive.

3. The purpose of the church was to integrate the physical, emotional, socio-economic, and spiritual needs of homeless women and help them achieve holistic salvation in contrast to the reality of service agencies, medical professions, and Christian churches that seem to divide a person into separate parts according to their problems and needs. This was based on the belief that the Christian Church must offer a profound ground of hope and healing in God by enhancing the woman's image. If many traditional churches contributed toward lowering a woman's image, the ministry of the Church of Mary Magdalene was to undo this damage.

4. The purpose was to meet the needs of homeless women who come from many different walks of life and religious backgrounds. The church was started as an **ecumenical** marching.

We had one solid goal of freeing homeless women from their suffering, abuse, and homelessness and leading them to a joyful dance as illustrated in the logo. My amazing experience with this church was a clear witness to

Pastor Jean and a member of
Church of Mary Magdalene

the fact that God transformed all my losses and traumas into compassion to serve the homeless people who were profoundly injured by losing everything—homes, jobs, families, children, friends, hopes, health (including their own minds)—just as I had. They were all sick in despair unto death just as I was. I could help them find hope, motivation to live, and get back to their lives. I could guide them to the opportunity to restore their self-esteem and the pride and dignity that they lost so that they could experience a positive, loving, forgiving God instead of the punishing, judging God they learned about in their abusive relationships.

I was already in a position of "wounded healer." So I was marching with them for seven years, which passed like seven months!! Therefore, all the wounds, hurts, pain, tragedy, illness, and loss can never bind us to the chain of despair forever, but they can become a strong foundation to do something good for yourself and others. So if we march together with God, everything is possible.

At the Church of Mary Magdalene, I highlighted **worship service and singing**. I brought singing spiritual songs from my own experience. When I lost my boy, whenever grief, guilt, and pain crushed and choked me and I could not breathe, I would sit down with a hymnal and begin to sing from the first page on. In my singing I would cry out, scream, groan, and mourn, plead, confess and pray.

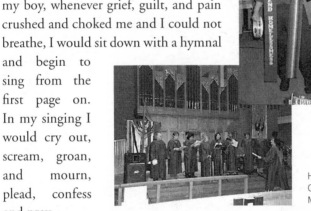

Homeless Women's Choir of the Church of Mary Magdalene.

By the time I reached the last page of the hymnal, I experienced relief and was able to breathe, got up to cook or went to work or went to bed to sleep. From this experience I learned that music can be a powerful instrument of God's healing.

So I invited my congregation to march with me in singing. Even a woman who was sick with catatonic schizophrenia and was frozen in her chair and never talked to anyone was shaking her head and body along with music and melody. She, too, was marching with the rest of the women. We shook scarves, tambourines, banged on drums, and whatever we could grab along with our marching. I, who never learned dancing, ended up dancing and marching with my women while singing. We sang emotionally, physically, and spiritually. Healthy women, sick women, angry women, depressed women all sang and marched together. Women experienced relief, joy, and peace after singing out all their frustration, anger, and depression. Women also witnessed that they could not be angry and sing at the same time. These women were a bundle of anger. However, singing was a very joyful experience. It was an amazing songfest! We experienced the presence of the Spirit and built a cohesive community among ourselves. They enjoyed it so much that no one wanted to stop singing even after an hour. So I had to stop them to proceed with the worship service and to meet the lunch schedule.

At one point, I did a little research on the impact of music. *Psychology Today* reports several research findings about the immediate psychological and medical benefits of music as follows:

Music increases happiness, less stress, reduced depressive symptoms, greater autonomy, and increased competence, hope, and optimism. Music offers an easy, natural way to relieve anxiety, increase alertness, feel happier, sharpen memory, improve mood, and fight off insomnia, depression and even addictions, without any side effects. Research shows that children who are involved with music programs grow up to have lower rates of addictive behaviors, better academic performance, and greater preparedness for college and the work force. Music making (playing an instrument or singing) is a multimodal activity that involves the integration of auditory and sensorimotor processes.[10] Music listening can enhance the emotional and cognitive functioning of patients affected by various neurological conditions. Intensive singing practice can lead to long-lasting effects in both the cardiovascular and pulmonary problems.[11] Because the act of singing requires long, repeated contractions of various respiratory muscles, this type of training may help to preserve the maximal expiratory pressure of patients with chronic obstructive pulmonary disease.[12]

Singing has been identified as having important therapeutic potential for individuals who stutter. [13] Several studies show the result that singing reduced the frequency of stuttering by more than 90 percent. It has

[10] Catherine Y. Wan et al.

[11] Grape, Sandgren, Hansson, Ericson, and Theorell, 2003.

[12] Bonilha et al., 2009.

[13] Healey, Mallard, and Adams, 1976.

been estimated that more than 80 percent of patients with Parkinson's disease develop voice and speech problems at some point. Research has shown that intensive voice therapy can be effective in reducing the speech abnormalities experienced by patients with Parkinson's disease.

Aphasia is a common and devastating complication of stroke or other brain injuries that results in the loss of the ability to produce and/or comprehend language. Research has shown that singing has been shown to produce improvements in chronic stroke patients. Autism can also potentially be helped by singing. Autism is characterized by impairments in expressive language and communication. Studies have described the positive effects of singing on the development of speech in children with autism. Singing reduces the risk of heart disease. They also found that the combination of physical activity while listening to your favorite music improved the lining of your blood vessels and showed impressive benefits on cardiovascular health. [14]

Mary Magdalene Choir in purple shirts

On top of all these good things, spiritual songs brought us closer to God, who also seemed to be singing and marching with us and helped us realize how deeply he loves us. We could confess "I have seen the Lord." Knowing all these, who wouldn't sing? I would sing and march instead of taking anti-depressants!

I experienced overwhelming joy when I saw women felt good about themselves, stopped abusing drugs and alcohol, found faith in God, and changed their life. Also, the women who were very obnoxious and threatening in the beginning have changed over the years and don't act that way anymore, as they feel better about themselves.

I took eleven choir members to Washington, DC. To make a long story short, I was invited to lead a workshop and our choir to sing at a national event.

---

[14] Christopher Bergland in The Athlete's Way, Published on September 2, 2013.

Choir of Church of Mary Magdalene in Washington, DC

On rainy days, we all were wearing rain coats and took a bus or walked. It was a life-changing experience for them to take a tour of the White House.

The name of the church came from the woman in the Bible whom Jesus freed from seven demons (Luke 8:2): She was healed as she marched with Jesus. I called the women's life experiences "multiple difficulties," including physical, emotional, mental illness, tragedy, abuse, and homelessness. The name was intended to offer hope for homeless women, so they could experience healing from their multiple difficulties and be healed like Mary Magdalene had been by marching with Jesus.

It was a conversational sermon in which the whole congregation participated: Most of these women had been preached at, pointed out as sinners, judged, and condemned in other worship settings. Preaching together not only met their spiritual needs, but also helped them feel important, because it was about their input rather than my preaching at them. I used to comment "You are better than biblical commentaries in your input, sharing and relating to my text so well."

The offering was also a healing ritual: Women were encouraged to write on a piece of paper all their negative and destructive feelings, problems, pains, burdens and habits, wrong doings and illness that they didn't want to own any more, and then bring the papers to God as their offering. We burnt them in a bowl as a proof that God took these offerings away and forgave them.

Shared prayers: Women participated in prayer for themselves, others, their nation and the world, and they felt closer to God. Amazing numbers of women called the names of their children who were in legal custody.

One well-known distinctive mission was the lingerie mission: A lingerie ministry was developed as a tangible way to help restore woman's dignity and pride. We offered a new clean pair of lingerie on a quarterly basis. Our women could seldom purchase new clothes, often wearing donated used clothes. Wearing unfitting, dirty, or used underwear, no one could feel like a person, especially women. I Cor. 3:16 says that "our body is the temple of God's spirit."

This means that we went beyond the spirituality to meet a variety of social needs: feeding, clothing bank, finding housing, crisis intervention, and becoming their moving truck, their taxi service, you name it. The logo, an affirmation of faith, litanies, worship, singing, and healing rituals were developed. We added weekly activities such as breakfast, hot lunch, Bible study, counseling sessions, housing/job searches, job training, arts and crafts, a simple food pantry, outreach, crisis intervention, a case management service, a medical/nursing service, massage, exercise, and many more services.

I developed a shirt that "End Homelessness for All Women" was printed on. I began to wear it in 1997 when I went to the General Assembly of the Presbyterian Church (U.S.A.) to receive the Women of Faith award and to pass an overture demanding every Presbyterian Church Open One Room to make it a shelter for the homeless. That time I printed my message in several different colors and wore them as I stood before the public. Later, I chose the color purple. To this day, I have been wearing the purple shirts day and night for seven days a week, perhaps in my cascade also.

These activities were all under one roof at The Church of Mary Magdalene as a day program that went on throughout the week. Now they put all these under the auspice of Mary's Place, which was the name of a previous day program. The following affirmation we recited at every worship service, and litany of women on Mother's Day because it was a very sad day for many, with lots of guilt for losing their children to Child Protective Service. They were also angry toward their parents and grown children. Therefore, we renamed Mother's Day as Women's Day. By reading the litany of women we uplifted the image of women.

The Holy Spirit marched with me by flying me for seven years of serving homeless women, literally carrying me on her back. It wasn't my power or my speed at all. This is another story of her marching with me. Therefore, it is God's story! God's marching with homeless women.

Worship at a Picnic: These women had no place to go. Therefore, I took them to a picnic four times during the summer. I got churches to sponsor our picnics by

Summer picnic of the Church of Mary Magdalene at Magnussen Park

the beach. It was at this point that I wrote Affirmation of faith and Litany of Women.

AFFIRMATION OF FAITH

We who are homeless or suffering from multiple difficulties, believe in God who created and blessed women and men equally in God's own image. We affirm God as a loving and forgiving God, not a condemning God. Therefore, we refuse to be treated as inferior and less-worthy human beings. We loudly affirm that we deserve to dream a vision, hope, and future. We re-imagine Jesus Christ as a forgiving and healing mother, father, sister, brother, friend, and Savior who, himself, was homeless, abused, and killed on a cross. We affirm Jesus's resurrection as a mirror of our own healing from our poverty, homelessness, brokenness, bondage, and destructive thoughts and actions. We affirm the Holy Spirit as our source of strength and inspiration who raises us after every fall. The Spirit constantly leads us back home to God. We affirm our gathering as a worshipping community that practices love, joy, peace, forgiveness, security, and support for one another. Amen.

LITANY OF WOMEN

W WOMAN is a <u>W</u>arm, <u>W</u>ise, <u>W</u>orthy, <u>W</u>onderful, <u>W</u>illing <u>W</u>inner.

O WOMAN is an <u>O</u>ptimistic, <u>O</u>vercoming and <u>O</u>rdained <u>O</u>ne by God.
WOMAN is an <u>O</u>wner of a womb that is a warm, welcoming,
wonderful place where life is conceived, loved, nurtured;
Woman can be an <u>O</u>pportunity for life for <u>O</u>thers.

M WOMAN is a blessed <u>M</u>other who is a <u>M</u>agnificent <u>M</u>agic <u>M</u>aker.

A WOMAN is an <u>A</u>ble and <u>A</u>ppreciative <u>A</u>ngel.
WOMAN is a loving <u>A</u>gent.

N WOMAN is a <u>N</u>eeded, <u>N</u>eat, <u>N</u>atural, <u>N</u>ice and <u>N</u>urturing person.
WOMAN offers <u>N</u>ew beginnings to all human beings.

Marching Sixtieth Birthday—Saturday, July 15, 1995

I celebrated my sixtieth birthday with my homeless sisters at Madrona Park in Seattle. My son cooked lots of good food and invited musician to play music all day. I had never seen my homeless sisters have that much fun. They were joyfully marching with music all day!

I told my friends not to bring any gifts for me. Instead, I was going to create a "no homeless night" in Seattle. At Christmas time I sent out volunteers to gather up as many homeless women as possible and put them in motel rooms. That whole year $10,000 came in. And

My 60th birthday party at Madrona Park

throughout the year I helped 187 homeless sisters and their children with rental assistance with the rest of the funds. Thanks to my generous friends.

Marching Women's Retreat

The purpose of this retreat was to develop women's leadership. Some women carried lots of potential to be leaders but didn't have a chance to cultivate their potential toward leadership. So one day, by the ocean, relaxing with good food and discussion, we discovered their talents and leadership possibilities so that they could participate in the mission not

just as recipients of services, but share their selves with other women. **So the lives of women and the ministry kept on marching. It has never stopped at one place because we all needed to grow together.**

Marching Retirement (Dec 1997)

I thought I could be dead in 1996 or 1997, because my asthmatic cough got worse when I was out on wet, cold, and windy Seattle streets all day doing outreach to lost souls; I **marched** through department store bathrooms, day drop-in centers, parks, libraries, emergency shelters, low-income apartments, clinic lobbies, etc. I was coughing to death, feeling and fearing that one night I might stop breathing.

I requested early retirement from my board at age sixty-two. We had over a year to prepare by hiring a new pastor. The cartoon image was a retirement gift for me in a frame that came with no explanation of the meaning. I almost fell out of my chair I was so shocked

when I first saw it! Who can express better the image of the homeless women's mission than this cartoon? The more years with my homeless mission have gone by, the closer I seem to get to the heart of the cartoon. The original came with the words "Jean walks on the water" underneath the cartoon. However, I didn't dare to keep it there.

The life that homeless people live and the mission I have been leading are so difficult that I adopted four Chinese characters to name it: "Chon Shin Man Ko" (as Koreans pronounce it), which literally means "a thousand hot peppers and ten thousand hardships," which I paraphrase as "a thousand pains and ten thousand troubles." Walking on the water without carrying anything would be hard enough. Walking on the water pulling a boat behind us would be harder, and even harder still would be walking on the water pulling a boat full of people.

千辛万苦

I would liken a difficult and impossible homeless life to pulling a boat on the water full of people onboard: I have observed that.

It is a huge struggle for anyone in this day and age to live through a homeless life, which is so brutal because they have to fight with their temporary/chronic physical/emotional/intellectual challenges, addictions, and bad habits; they have to fight with financial and employment barriers, past rental and legal history, and current skyrocketing unaffordable housing; they have to fight with tons of tickets for traffic violations, public drinking, loitering, smoking, and sleeping outdoors; they have to fight with unfriendly police and ordinances that show little mercy to the homeless; they have to fight with all the stumbling blocks from their past incarceration history, eviction history, debts for apartments, and even to the federal government for college tuition; they have to fight with the shelter, and social service system, and

Retirement worship with homeless women and their choir in purple shirts

low-income housing; they have to fight for food, sleeping, parking spots, restrooms, and showers every day and night; fight the temptation to drink or use drugs, and drop out of college and life all together. They must fight with cold/wet/freezing weather; and fight with robbery, violence, and assault in their street life.

Therefore, homeless life is "a fight, struggle, and impossible task," just as pulling a boat on the water full of people onboard is. And so is the mission serving these people! Could that be the meaning of the cartoon?

On my retirement day, these women gave me gifts of a plaque and albums full of their photos and affectionate words.

CHAPTER 29

Marching
Presbyterian Initiative

In 1997, I happened to go to General Assembly (the national gathering of the Presbyterian Churches) to receive a Women of Faith award. It happened to be the year that the overture from Seattle Presbytery was being presented.

I made homeless shirts as the photo shows in different colors and wore them to demonstrate my message because each one of us was given only three minutes to speak.

After the General Assembly adopted an overture to "end homelessness for women and children" in 1997 and 1998, which became a Presbyterian initiative that was to move into action by the Women's Ministries Program Area (the director was Rev. Barbara Dua) of the Presbyterian Church (U.S.A.).

The initiatives include the following resolutions:

1. Every church opens at least one room for ministry to the poor and homeless.

2. Urge Presbyterian congregations to work cooperatively with other churches, religious groups, and charitable or governmental entities to help provide safe and secure shelter for homeless women in times of crisis.

3. Call upon Presbyterian churches to work with policymakers to create fair and just economic and housing policies, and to create funding to implement those policies.

4. Encourage Presbyterians to wear the homeless shirts and spread the message to end homelessness for all women and children throughout the nation.

A shirt drive was approved, with the message "End Homelessness for All Women" or "All People" printed on the shirts as our national campaign.

Marching Presbyterian Women's Ministry

A couple of months prior to my retirement from the Church of Mary Magdalene, September 1997, I happened to lead a workshop at the National Presbyterian Welfare Consultation in Louisville. Barbara Dua, then associate director of the Women's Ministries Program Area of the national General Assembly Presbyterian office, was one of my workshop participants whom I did not know at the time.

Women's Ministries
On Behalf of Women!

Rev. Barbara Dua writes, "As the new associate director of Women's Ministries, I had been considering for several months what direction God might be suggesting for the women's ministries program area. During the night after attending Jean Kim's workshop, I had a dream. It was such a powerful dream that it awakened me. I sat up in bed and rehearsed the dream in my mind. Then it became clear to me, in some mysterious way, I felt that I must talk with Jean Kim to see if it might be possible that her call to challenge the church in concrete ways to end homelessness might be a program from Women's Ministries. Feminist theology could be put into action in an important way as we served the often voiceless and marginalized among us. The following day Jean Kim and I talked, and it was clear to both of us that her sense of call to the larger faith community and my sense of God's direction for Women's Ministries could be realized in her joining our staff with this mission before us." (from the Foreword, Jubilee Manual, 2000).

Hearing about my retirement, she offered me a short-term (two years) speaking tour job. Although the above statement was true, I didn't know what to do with the job offer because I wasn't looking for another job, as I was preparing to die. When she called me a week later to ask if I had decided to accept the job offer, I took it as God's lead to another call; this time it was very clear, concrete and loud. Since I surrendered to God to do anything **God wants to do with me** I was compelled to say yes. The job was traveling around the whole nation to motivate Presbyterians to do something toward ending homelessness. So Presbyterian Church (U.S.A.) hired me to be an associate who is responsible for educating the presbyteries and congregations throughout the nation on the issue of homelessness. I didn't look for it . . . I didn't ask for it. **I wasn't even qualified to do it.** It just came as a gift from God.

Marching on the Road

So my marching on the road started. I was so excited!! To make a long story short, I felt very humble and even ashamed to be a bold speaker with only a nickel's worth of ideas and experience on "homelessness."

The homeless mission programs I visited in the nation taught me so much that I was indebted to all them. Later, this experience became one five volumes written in hopes that it would be a useful tool, not because of what I say but because it contains over 133 wonderful model programs visited. (Ref: Vol. 4, Purple People, www.jeankimhome.com.) All of them appeared to be the miracle works of the Holy Spirit, who constantly empowers good chosen people to carry out the program for our Lord, Jesus Christ.

During my marching on the road, my asthma even got better. My knees that collapsed on my marching road also got better and I could walk very fast without crutches!

Reflecting upon the ministry of homeless women in Seattle and speaking to Presbyterians to end homelessness all meant "planting a cross," as God commanded me to do; planting the hope, love, and forgiveness, of Jesus Christ in the souls of homeless women and planting the value, life, and commandment of Jesus Christ to love our neighbor as ourselves in the hearts of the Presbyterians. We all are called to plant the cross, Jesus himself in everyone's soul and life.

Staff at the National Women's Ministries program area.

Thus, Rev. Barbara Dua helped housed Presbyterian women in the nation to march along with purple homeless women. To achieve the goal, the Reverend Barbara Dua, then the director of the Women's Ministries program area, hired me, which I hadn't dare to dream could happen. Although it was the denominational initiative, I was already carrying it deep in my heart. And thus, I was excited about the unexpected call and was ready to roll.

At first, however, I was anxious, thinking, "What if no one invites me to speak?" Publicity went out through Presbyterian women's newsletters and other publications. Words got around. To my surprise, invitations began to pour in for speaking engagements.

On February 1, 1998, on behalf of the Women's Ministries program area, I began to travel, raising consciousness, motivating, educating, and resourcing, and challenging Presbyterians to develop homeless ministries to end homelessness for women and children in the United States. In those days, I was serving homeless women and children. I was shocked to see so many of them on the streets and was highly motivated to awaken Presbyterian congregations toward ending their homelessness. However, without the support of colleagues in the Women's Ministries Program, I couldn't have done it.

At the 1998 General Assembly's exhibition hall, the Women's Ministries program area and Presbyterian women highlighted building one room in the church with cardboard blocks to encourage churches to host homeless women and children.

In fact, I designed the 1997 and 1998 Presbyterian resolutions to end homelessness to help Churches in Seattle Presbytery to prepare to submit overtures to the Presbytery through which overtures can be submitted to the National Assembly. I feel grateful and fortunate that articles I authored went all the way up to the national level to encourage the whole church to participate in action together toward ending homelessness in the U.S.

Marching in Purple Shirts

Because it was for the national Women's Ministries Program of the Presbyterian Church (U.S.A.), "End Homelessness for All Women" needed to be printed on the shirt. And it also carried the *"every church open one room"* initiative along with it.

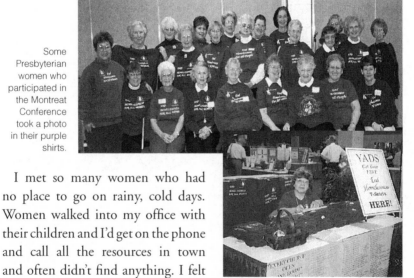

Some Presbyterian women who participated in the Montreat Conference took a photo in their purple shirts.

I met so many women who had no place to go on rainy, cold days. Women walked into my office with their children and I'd get on the phone and call all the resources in town and often didn't find anything. I felt helpless and frustrated. I thought, "I can't do this anymore. I've got to do something to change the system."

I brought a box of homeless shirts to every conference. Many Presbyterians wore these shirts nationwide.

So I worked with Seattle Presbytery to move the General Assembly of the Presbyterian Church (U.S.A.) to adopt a policy to end homelessness for all women! The movement was an earthshaking outcry to end the pain of women's homelessness. I also developed a shirt campaign to spread the message fast, this time in purple, the color of Lent. I already mentioned at the beginning why my color is purple. Ending homelessness is so important because in this affluent nation it does not make any sense to have so many people left in homelessness. God may not forgive us for that. For women to be homeless, children to be homeless . . . children being homeless means homelessness of our future generation in this country, and homelessness of our future generation means hopelessness of this nation. So we have to end it!!

My conviction is that God wants us to do this. Churches have been giving us material support, prayer, and emotional support—wonderful!! Without them we could not have a mission program . . . but I was urging all the churches to move beyond that. I wanted them to join the "End Homelessness" movement. So I was also asking the churches to empty one room and accept homeless people. This room can be used for transitional housing, emergency housing, or a respite bed for the sick. It can be a training center, job search center, daycare for welfare mothers, or a school for homeless kids. Food bank, clothing bank. I have a list of

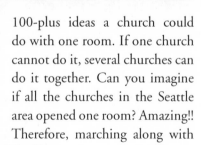

100-plus ideas a church could do with one room. If one church cannot do it, several churches can do it together. Can you imagine if all the churches in the Seattle area opened one room? Amazing!! Therefore, marching along with homeless purple women is possible and doable.

Horizons magazine's September-October 1998 issue included the photo and story and once again emphasized the "every church open one room"

campaign, which was the call of the overture. *"Jean Kim, associate for ending the homelessness of women, Women's Ministries Area, sits inside a room built by visitors to the Charlotte Convention Center exhibit hall during the 1998 General Assembly. The room symbolizes space devoted to the care of homeless people; the 'bricks' are labeled with ideas for homeless ministry."*

The year 2000 Presbyterian Women's Statewide Gathering gave half of the offering to two homeless women's projects in the nation and used homeless litanies for worship service and allowed me to address the whole group for generous offerings. I am grateful to the five thousand Presbyterian women who gave so generously that the total offering amounted to $87,000, which was the highest the Presbyterian Women ever gathered at one conference. The loud outcry of the homeless initiative was echoed through the ears and the hearts of all the participants.

In 1998 and 1999, I worked full time for the Women's Ministries. In two years, I spoke to one hundred and eighty-seven groups in nineteen different cities boarding one hundred and eight planes.

Marching Presbyterian Hunger Program

I would say that hunger and homelessness are the twin children of poverty:
After I worked for the Women's Ministries program area for two years, the Presbyterian Hunger Program inherited me in 2000 with the vision of the "Ending Homelessness Initiative," which continued through December 2003. Many hungry people are homeless and most homeless people  experience hunger not only physical but in every aspect of life. Hunger and homelessness are caused by poverty.

Jean Kim's "End Homelessness"

From the beginning I began to write my own handouts on the issue of homelessness, which turned into 200-page resource. I am grateful that the Hunger Program published the material under the title *"Jean Kim's End Homelessness."* I added "Jubilee Manual" as a subtitle because it was written in the year 2000, when the Presbyterian Women were celebrating jubilee and the whole purpose of the initiative was to liberate people from

hunger, poverty, and homelessness. The book includes seventy-seven ways that churches can help and one hundred and twenty-seven program examples I visited throughout the nation in two years. I used to make people laugh by saying *"if any church cannot do any of the seventy-seven ways, they may go to see a psychiatrist."* The Hunger Program edited my casual talk into a twenty-minute video and distributed it to the whole church.

The Hunger Program also inherited the T-shirt drive, replacing the logo of the Church of Mary Magdalene that I started in Seattle with the logo of the Presbyterian Church (U.S.A.). The Hunger Program sold these three items through the Presbyterian Distribution Center to serve as resources for the whole church. Without the support from the staff and Rev. Gary Cook, the coordinator of the Hunger Program, I couldn't have done it!

Foreword by Rev. Gary R. Cook

I remember seeing, as a child, old newsreel images of breadlines and soup kitchens—realities that I was comfortably assured belonged in the long-past Great Depression. It is one of my greatest disappointments in life (and in my country) that my children have now grown to adulthood thinking of soup kitchens and homeless shelters as a normal part of American life.

In a time of unprecedented economic strength, it should not be this way, but there is a growing segment of our population to whom the benefits of prosperity have never trickled down. The rising economic tide that was to "float all ships," has left many of our sisters and brothers swamped in poverty, hunger, and homelessness.

How the church responds to this situation says much about our true commitment to the Christ who identified directly with the poor and the marginalized. Do we look the other way? Do we cast a disapproving glance? Do we exempt ourselves from concern because of our busy-ness or because the problems are "too complicated"? Or do we find ways to join Jesus in reaching out to the "untouchables" of our society? Jean Kim has chosen to follow Jesus. And in two years of traveling across the United States, she has found many Presbyterian congregations who have chosen that route as well. Drawing from her many years of experience and the inspiring stories of programs she has visited, Jean shares her learnings and her commitments in this Jubilee Manual, which the Presbyterian Hunger Program is pleased to make available to the church.

As Jean points out, provision of services to homeless people, no matter how lovingly they are provided, is only part of the needed response to homelessness. We also need to ask "why?" "Why are so many people left out or left behind in this era of prosperity?" "Why are so many people with jobs numbered among the homeless?" "Why has our government passed laws that exacerbate the problems and at the same time discontinued programs that help prevent or remedy homelessness?" I invite you to join the Presbyterian Hunger Program and many Christians across the country in seeking answers to these questions—and an alternative public response that begins to put an end to homelessness.

It is my prayer that my children's children will grow up in a world where widespread soup kitchens and homeless shelters are once again relics of the past. Until that day, I give thanks for the efforts of faithful Christians who reach out in the name of Jesus to provide shelter, food, and hope to those in need.[15]

Gary R. Cook
Associate for National Hunger Concerns
Presbyterian Hunger Program
World Ministries Division, Presbyterian Church (U.S.A.)

Foreword by Rev. Barbara Dua

"Do you know where to find Jesus?" asks the small, five-foot-tall pastor, the Reverend Jean Kim. After a pause, she boldly states, "Jesus is on the

---

[15] Jean Kim, *Jean Kim's End Homelessness. Jubilee Manual*

streets. Jesus is homeless. If you go to the streets, there, you will find Jesus!" My dear friend Jean Kim knows where to find Jesus. Finding Jesus so often in the bruised face of a homeless woman, perhaps the victim of years of domestic violence, or in the eyes of a young mother who turned to selling her body as a way to provide food for her young children, Jean Kim discovered a basic search within us all for a home. Jean Kim learned that we seek that place of belonging and being loved as a valuable child of God, emotionally, spiritually, but also, physically. God's dream that we all live "at home," was the call to Rev. Kim to begin a church for homeless women in Seattle. This church, The Church of Mary Magdalene, has become a spiritual home for hundreds of women and from this faith-based center, emotional and physical needs have been met for thousands of homeless women over the past thirteen years.

In 1997, I had the privilege as the associate director for Women's Ministries to present Jean Kim with one of the three annual Women of Faith awards at the General Assembly in Syracuse, New York. While this award is known as a great honor in the Presbyterian Church (U.S.A.), and recipients often come to the celebration breakfast in their finest attire, Rev. Kim received her award in her daily uniform of purple running pants and a purple sweatshirt that reads, "End Homelessness for All Women." Rev. Kim lives her commitment to ending homelessness every day, all day, and even her clothing is a witness to the call she received from God. Several months after the Women of Faith award ceremony, I had the opportunity to attend a workshop Rev. Kim led on ending homelessness. During this workshop Jean mentioned that she was retiring after ten years as pastor of the Church of Mary Magdalene. She said that she felt God was calling her beyond the Seattle streets to spread the urgent word that people of faith must respond to this national disgrace. She also said that while she had no idea what she would be doing next, and even though she was in her sixties and not able or ready to retire, she was confident that God would show her where this new call would lead her.

As the new associate director of Women's Ministries, I had been considering for several months what direction God might be suggesting for the Women's Ministries program area. During the night, after attending Jean Kim's workshop, I had a dream. It was such a powerful dream that it awakened me. I sat up in bed and rehearsed the dream in my mind.

Then it became clear to me, in some mysterious way, I felt that I must talk with Jean Kim to see if it might be possible that her call to challenge the church in concrete ways to end homelessness might be a program from Women's Ministries. Feminist theology could be put into action in an important way as we served the often voiceless and marginalized among us. The following day Jean Kim and I talked, and it was clear to both of us that her sense of call to the larger faith community and my sense of God's direction for Women's Ministries could be realized in her joining our staff with this mission before us. Over the past two and a half years, Jean Kim traveled endlessly, visiting churches, shelters, homeless programs, and soup kitchens. From coast to coast Rev. Kim took her message of ending homelessness and offered concrete ways every Presbyterian Church could participate by offering one room in each church to be used for child care, job training, health assistance, shelter, etc. Her proposal was simple, "every church, one room." As she preached from church to church she would look out at the congregation and ask, "How many rooms are in your church buildings?" When it was obvious no one knew, she would encourage this thought, "If you do not even know how many rooms you have, surely one could be put to use to end homelessness!"

Many churches, presbyteries, and women's groups and individuals have heard Rev. Kim's challenge and have responded in creative ways. Jean has visited many of these new initiatives to end homelessness as well as the many existing programs she visited on her travels these past few years. This book is the result of her call to accept God's dream that there are ways to end homelessness. We are people of hope and God has given us the abilities to work creatively in communities of faith to offer a home for every one of God's children. As you read this book and discover the many incredible ways Presbyterians are responding to this urgent need of our time, I invite you to participate not merely as a detached reader, but to allow Jean's experience to work within you. I believe Jean is right, that if our churches go into the streets, we will find Jesus. I conclude this forward with deep gratitude for the inspiring and hope-filled ministry of my colleague and friend the Reverend Jean Kim.

Barbara E. Dua
Former Associate Director
Women's Ministries Program Area

Foreword by Rev. and Mrs. Bill Cate

The Reverend Jean Kim's experience working with homeless people and the issues of homelessness has resulted in an essay of theological insight presenting models of action that reveal the ultimate in understanding of the responsibility of being a Christian in today's world. The entire study is set in the context of biblical concepts and basic Christian theological understandings. We are never at a loss as to the motivating dynamic that moves Jean Kim in mission.

Jean Kim's own personal experience of homelessness occurred when as a young girl she and her family escaped from North Korea, working their way down to South Korea, walking many nights through conflict zones. She became a refugee in South Korea moving from room to room for four years until the Korean War broke out. During the Korean War, her family became homeless in exile, escaping from the war zone. Arriving in Pusan, they slept in the train station parking lot for the first few nights until an old man offered his yard. Six members of her family stayed in an 8x8 makeshift shack on the yard patched by sheets, ration boxes, and a few pieces of panels for three years until the war was over.

In later life, her training as a social worker, as well as a theologian, has prepared her well for the pioneering work she has done with the homeless community. An important part of this book is her analysis of the many ways a congregation and concerned individuals can use the resources available to them to alleviate homelessness in their community. No one can say after reading this book, "What can I do about homelessness?"

Her actual case studies in the last portion of the book are an essential resource. She not only describes the ministry in detail, but she gives you references to call with telephone numbers and mailing addresses. She artfully combines the theological and biblical mandate with concrete action steps. Every church should have this manual in its library as well as all theological libraries in seminaries training our future religious leaders.

Rev. Dr. William B. Cate
President Director Emeritus
Church Council of Greater Seattle

Dr. Janice P. Cate
Feminist and Social Activist

In six years of speaking tours, I have spoken to 430 groups (small and large) in 96 different cities and 31 different states boarding planes 184 times. My confession is that unless God carried me on her back and marched along with me, this kind of marching on the road couldn't have been possible!

YEAR	Employment Status	Spoke to	Note	Total % of All Groups	No of Trips
1998	Full time	72 groups	7 Korean-speaking groups	10%	50 trips
1999	Full time	125 groups	14 Korean-speaking groups	12%	58 trips
2000	1/2 time	55 groups	15 Korean-speaking groups	27%	20 trips
2001	1/4 time	60 groups	33 Korean-speaking groups	55%	15 trips
2002	1/4 time	75 groups	20 Korean-speaking groups	27%	21 trips
2003	1/4 time	43 groups	11 Korean-speaking groups	26%	20 trips
TOTAL		**430 groups**	**101 Korean-speaking groups**	**23%**	**184 trips**

Marching Hostesses

From the beginning I was determined to stay with families while I was on a speaking tour. The purpose was three-fold: 1) I wanted to stand in solidarity with homeless people by living a simple life—not in luxurious hotels. 2) I wanted to build close relationships with hosts/hostesses by sharing their housing and meals. 3) It was a way of saving money for

the programs I was working for because I used to spend more than the travel budget allowed due to the high demand for me to speak. And therefore, it wasn't hard to find host families when they understood such motives. Besides, they were marching along with me and the purple women's initiates.

I went to Point Barrow, Alaska to speak to the Presbyterian Church there. As the photo shows, I am standing below the jawbone of a whale. I could hardly imagine the size of the whale! With a jaw that size, the fish could swallow three Jonahs! It was November, but the Arctic Ocean was freezing in.

Had I stayed in hotels, the financial burden would have been great for the programs I worked for and for the hosting parties that invited me. we added up the cost for lodging with meals and local transportation that host families provided the figure would have been paramount.

My hosts in Niagara Falls, New York

Moreover, the host families became wonderful mission partners due to the close relationship we developed even in a short time. When we share housing and meals it binds the relationship closer and deeper. There are many such stories in the Bible when Jesus shared meals with the poor or rich, the relationship deepened, and their eyes were open for new visions.

And therefore, the Women's Ministries program area and the Hunger Program are deeply indebted to one hundred and sixteen hosts for their warm hospitality for me. These hosts also marched along with me and the purple people.

I am so grateful to those who offered me warm hospitality with a free room and board and local transportation as well while I was on my marching tour. It was a very enriching experience to share their homes and culture. I remember every one of them by name and their home environments. I treasure my relationships with them, gifts from God that no one can erase from my heart.

Although some of them moved or retired, I feel they are the true partners of the initiative, who helped us carry out the mission. Without their partnership, reaching out to 430 groups in 31 states wouldn't have been possible. I hope the whole denomination of the Presbyterian Church (U.S.A.) will join me in saluting them all.

Marching Korean American Churches

With help from the Holy Spirit, gradually the number of Korean American congregations increased (as shown in the chart earlier), with interest in the initiative to end homelessness. The initiative awakened many Korean American congregations that have been deeply involved with overseas missions rather than local missions.

Pre-Conference

In partnership with the National Council of Korean Presbyterian Churches (U.S.A.), the hunger program allowed me to offer a pre-conference the day before the national conference mainly inviting Korean American Presbyterian pastors. Since we gave subsidies for one hotel night and a meal, response was great. Later, invitations for me to visit their churches came in and they were included in the national campaign to end homelessness. I have done this pre-conference for four to five years. As I completed this special mission I was awarded a plaque of appreciation and was invited to preach for one evening's service during the national conference. During and after this pre-conference I visited homeless missions run by Korean Americans. Later, I visited their mission sites quite regularly every year.

Marching KACH
(Korean American Coalition for the Homeless)

As we ended the pre-conference in 2005, we formed the Korean American Coalition for the Homeless (KACH) among Korean-speaking service agencies, churches, and individuals. Thus, one national mission program came into being. This group elected me as the first chair for two years to set the tone and then leadership was rotated to other members.

The KACH is organized exclusively for charitable purposes, more specifically to participate in the national effort to end homelessness. Most Korean American mission leaders carry out this difficult mission in isolated and lonely circumstances. Therefore, another purpose of KACH was to encourage and comfort one another, learn from each other's experience, and help solicit support in each area where our Korean

American leaders carry out homeless missions. Each year the annual meeting moves around to a different city where KACH members are sharing resources and soliciting financial support from the area churches. Each participating mission group shares its particular way of carrying out missions. This is where KACH members as well as the local churches learn from different homeless missions in the nation. They appreciate seeing Korean American–led Homeless missions in the United States.

Under the auspices of KACH, I got to visit several homeless missions that were carried out by Korean American leaders. Here are some sample:

Marching New Haven Homeless (Connecticut)

Purple people and faith communities in New Haven marched along with Seattle purple people! The following is a speech I gave on the tenth anniversary of Agape Church.

I am nobody, but dare to name myself "a mother, coworker, adviser, and a cofounder" of Agape Church. And I may reflect upon the Agape history as follows: One day, Jackie Yu told me that because of her attendance at my workshops on homelessness five times, she was motivated to start a homeless mission in the New Haven area. Thus, I flew to New Haven. On a rainy cold day, I took Jackie to a small tent city on a church lawn in downtown New Haven to show her how to start a mission. We greeted a few homeless friends there and invited them to our breakfast to learn about the homeless situation in the New Haven area. They taught us all about it. That could have been the moment when the Agape Church was conceived. We then invited them to be our friends and partners for our new mission for the homeless. Jackie and I visited several churches in the area for a space, with no success. I left for Seattle leaving Jackie with a plan for how to befriend and serve the homeless people who are sitting in the area parks as much as she could afford, and she would continue to contact churches for a space. Later I heard Trinity Lutheran Church offered a space for their spiritual home. We praised the Lord. Trinity was a God-sent angel!

To model after God's agape (unconditional love), I suggested "Agape Church" for the mission's name. No one challenged that name and it became the name of the church. Jackie Yu and Si Young organized the first board. I helped apply to the Connecticut State Government to register Agape Church as a non-profit. Except for a few recent years, I have flown to New Haven every year, preached at many Korean- and English-speaking churches to thank them for their past support and solicit more future support. Jackie and I consulted over the phone hundreds of times when I couldn't be there physically.

The first few years were full of hardships and afflictions for Jackie. Rev. Sang Jin Choi in Washington, DC, and I flew to New Haven to support and comfort her.

But she reported she was experiencing more stress from churches than support, and finally announced that she was giving it up. I flew to New Haven to revive stress-stricken Jackie. First, I revived the Connecticut non-profit status, which was being cancelled. We decided to file for 501(C)

Sometimes they worship at a park next to Yale University. Un Chu Yu (second from the left), leader of the Agape Church.)

(3) tax exempt status to encourage tax-deductible contributions. In those days, the only financial resource was Si Young's wallet. We had no money to hire a lawyer, therefore, I decided to prepare the long, many-page documents of the 501(C)(3) application myself. I couldn't stay in New Haven too long and returned home, gathering up information from Agape board members and Jackie over the phone. I had to learn how to do it by asking hundreds of questions of everyone I met, including federal IRS staff. It was like writing a doctoral dissertation, but I finally got the paperwork together and submitted it. We were so happy and jumped for joy when we got the 501(C)(3) status approval. Jackie Yu was re-energized, rose from her despair, and started to march and serve all over again. After that, Sang Jin Choi and I, being representatives of the Korean American Coalition for the Homeless, held a ceremony to commission

Jackie Yu as our missionary for Agape Church. Ever since she has been called "Missionary Jackie."

For the first ten years, Jackie had been an unpaid mother for the homeless on the New Haven streets. Her purse was stolen several times by those whom she was serving. She found jobs for the homeless and went to work with them. She acted as a landlord for them to help them pay rent on time whenever she put them into housing. She helped get vendor licenses for homeless brothers to earn something. She became the manager of their funds by opening a savings account for them. She visited factories and markets to gather up food and clothes for them. From dawn till dark, she worked so hard that her back was often literally bent with pain. Too frequently her husband was left with no dinner but ramen noodles. With no private life, her first ten years were filled with tears, hard work, a broken heart, and stress, but also with never-ceasing love for the homeless and God with all her heart, soul, and might, and the great joy of serving them.

When the Korean churches put her down, the Connecticut governor lifted her up with an award. When churches closed doors on her face, God opened heaven's gate and sent her more supporters. The last few years Jackie has been crying out to heaven and earth for a space to open a day center for those who are not allowed even to sit on the streets. God heard her heartbreaking outcry and opened heaven's gate once again and poured out blessings through the United Church on the Green— free of charge. This is the heart of God. While the world sees her outer image, God was seeing her innermost depth of love for the homeless and responded accordingly. There seems to be no power under the sun to stop God's mighty power and love. God shared all her heartaches and acted on her behalf. Therefore, we human brings haven't done anything. It was all God's power and free grace marching with us.

Therefore, today, we are witness to God's wonderful gifts. Personally, I extend my love, thanks, and pride in Jackie who is my daughter/sister and God's daughter. Today we all give thanks to God who guided us, walked beside us, lifted us up, pushed us from behind, and ordained us from above. For many years to come until we have no more homeless in this land, I plead with you all to work together and support the Agape Church. I also pray that God's heavenly gate may stay wide open to shower abundant blessings upon those who support Agape Church, and upon churches that open their spaces for the homeless members of Agape Church, and upon their families, upon their children, upon their works, and upon the churches they serve, and upon all homeless brothers and sisters as always and evermore. Amen.

Thus, New Haven people and churches joined in marching along with the other purple people. It has been possible and doable!

Marching Chicago Homeless
House of Prayer for All the Nations (HOPAN)

As I mentioned above, HOPAN is another wonderful mission that is run by a Korean American pastor. So HOPAN was included in my regular visit, which I call "marching with Chicago homeless." And Rev. Kim's residence became my home in Chicago where I could comfortably stay while I visit his homeless church. I used to preach when I was there and met with many members and got to know them very well.

The name, "House of Prayer for all the Nations" comes from Mark 11:17. Jesus was teaching and saying, "Is it not written, 'My house shall be called *a house of prayer for all the nations?*'" which Jesus quoted from Isaiah 56:7. "All the nations" means all God's people of any color, nationality, culture, and economic status who are welcomed to experience a loving environment where there is no racial, economic and class discrimination.

Participants freely experience God's presence through prayer by the leader and for each other among participants, and soul-shaking gospel songs and worship. This experience brings not only spiritual transformation of their souls but also lifestyle change toward a much more responsible and productive life. HOPAN is organized by Korean American Christian Church leaders and lay people in Chicago to respond to the growing crisis of homelessness in the wider Chicago area. The purpose of the HOPAN was to develop a house of prayer and worship for all homeless people in order to guide them to God to restore, rehabilitate, and save their wounded souls and their lost dignity and also promote spiritual, emotional, and physical wellness. Such spiritual mission will also accompany meeting their physical and social human needs so that they can become respectful, self-sufficient, productive citizens of the state of Illinois and the United States.

HOPAN was also designed to challenge and educate local Korean American churches and the church as a whole on the reality and root causes of homelessness, guide them to love and serve homeless people in partnership with secular and government groups, and motivate them to participate in the local and national effort to end homelessness. HOPAN was conceived to build a network with national and local organizations that share the same values and goals.

Direct and indirect services of HOPAN to achieve the above goals may include but are not limited to:

- Development of a Christian Church for the homeless to offer an ecumenical Christian worship services with prayer, singing, Bible study, communion, and baptism
- Fellowship with free meals
- Food and clothing
- Health care services and education
- Legal assistance and education
- Life-skill and leadership training
- Job training and job search assistance
- Help finding low income/affordable housing
- Providing information, resources, and referral services
- Advocacy for the homeless and many more as needed

Marching Washington, DC Homeless (APPA)

When I was in the Washington, DC area to speak to a certain church group I heard that Rev. Choi had started a homeless mission in a tough area of DC. I needed to support him because he was doing this all alone. People who knew I was there told Rev. Choi, "You need to see Rev. Jean Kim, who is from the national office of the Presbyterian Church (U.S.A.)." Such encouragement and urging finally guided us to meet. I visited his center, which was set up in a free two-story home by a Korean Church in the area. Upstairs, people could sleep and downstairs, worship and dinner could be shared on Sundays. I remember hearing that the area was so tough that people had been shot and killed there. But ever since APPA came into being, the killing stopped.

Ever since, when I was in DC or Maryland, visiting this site was included in my travel schedule. Again, it became my home in the DC area.

The history of the APPA: The Action for Peace through Prayer and Aid (APPA) was founded in 1996 by Rev. Sang-Jin Choi

in Washington, DC. APPA is a United Nations–affiliated international organization located in Washington, DC and New York. It serves as an international leadership center working to end poverty and fostering racial harmony affiliated with the U.N.'s Economic and Social Council. There are various outreach programs offered to homeless and low-income persons, these include: food service, clothing service, family counseling, free legal counseling service, medical service, farm project, after-school programs for children, and a variety of social events for the community to enjoy as a whole. APPA has recently expanded its scope of assistance to downtown Baltimore, Maryland; New York; New Jersey; and Atlanta, Georgia, in the U.S., as well as Seoul, South Korea, and Volgograd, Russia.

Marching National Network

Thus, the mission of carrying out the Initiative moves one step forward by birthing the network. A committee was organized to form a Presbyterian Network to End Homelessness, under the sponsorship of the Presbyterian Hunger Program. The committee met twice in Chicago and finally gave birth to the Presbyterian Network to End Homelessness that started in January 2004 and committed people kept the torch burning up to this date. After my retirement from the speaking tour, I served as an interim director for one year.

The purpose of the network is:

1. To create a national network that will empower local ministries to end homelessness
2. To motivate, educate, train, and challenge Presbyterian congregations to respond, with their human and material resources, to God's call to end homelessness for millions of men, women and children in the U.S.

3. To support the Presbyterian Church as a denomination to keep alive the vision of the earlier General Assemblies and the work begun by the Women's Ministries program area and the Hunger Program

4. To respond to rising poverty and homelessness in such a time as this, when three million people have lost jobs in three years and a million people, especially families with children, are forced every night to be in homelessness

5. To promote the development of low-income housing that will result in bringing many Americans home

6. To deal with the root causes of increasing homelessness and respond collectively to eliminate them and to live out the will of our Lord Jesus Christ for justice for the poor

7. To promote public policies, at the local, state, and national levels, that respond creatively to both the needs of homeless people and the underlying issues of poverty and lack of affordable housing which contribute to them homelessness

These goals will be met through consultations, resourcing, networking, and outreach to synods, presbyteries, congregations, and other groups, as well as through annual national and regional training conferences.

Marching Retirement

The Night of Retirement Party from six years of the speaking tour. People

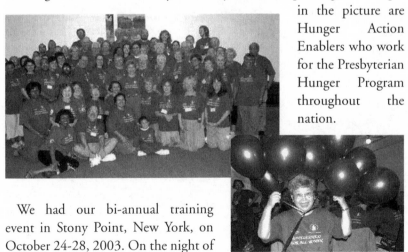 in the picture are Hunger Action Enablers who work for the Presbyterian Hunger Program throughout the nation.

We had our bi-annual training event in Stony Point, New York, on October 24-28, 2003. On the night of

the marching retirement party, fifty Hunger Action Enablers surprised and shocked me in preparing the farewell party by all wearing purple shirts and decorating everything—plates, napkins, cups and balloons—in purple. They couldn't have given me a better farewell party. It was the best one in the world and something that I never could have imagined or expected.

The Hunger Program staff, volunteers, and Hunger Action Enablers all are wonderful people who marched along with me. Without the support of the staff, especially the coordinator Rev. Gary Cook, I couldn't' have done it. So we always have a good crowd that marches with us. We are never alone!

They shipped purple shirts from the Louisville, Kentucky, Presbyterian Headquarter to Stony Point, New York, just for this farewell party for me. I owe them a huge thanks for this effort. I am in the center of the second row. Thank you, Gary, forever for your brilliant idea and care and love for your staff and colleagues.

So the Hunger Program and its enablers did march along with the purple people everywhere in the nation! It was possible and doable!

I called this marching retirement because I will keep marching on with the purple people after this retirement as I have done with other retirement.

Final Reflection on the Speaking Tour

I am sharing here my Final Reflection of serving General Assembly as Associate for ending homelessness for Women's Ministries program area and Hunger Program of Presbyterian Church (U.S.A.) for the period of February 1998 through December 2003, which reveals am amazing experience in abundance grace of God:

I am grateful to the grace of God, who inspired, guided, and used me for such an important mission as the "Ending Homelessness" initiative. I am grateful to Jesus Christ, who has been the model of the best host welcoming the poor, sick, and homeless.

I am grateful to the Presbyterian Church (U.S.A.), which adopted overtures (97-51 and 98-55) during the 209th and 210th General Assemblies in 1997 and 1998 to "end homelessness for all women and children" as a denominational policy, both of which were submitted

by the Seattle Presbytery and resulted in the "Ending Homelessness" initiative" for which I was gratefully called.

I am grateful to Rev. Barbara Dua, then assistant director of the Women's Ministries program area, of the Presbyterian Church (U.S.A.), for having the vision to include the overture to "end homelessness for women and children" as a mission of the Women's Ministries program area.

I am grateful to Rev. Gary Cook, who joined the "Ending Homelessness" initiative from the early stage and finally inherited the initiative and kept it alive through December 2003 and played the role of midwife in giving birth to the "Presbyterian Network End Homelessness." *Hunger and homelessness are the twin children of poverty.*

I am grateful to Presbyterian Urban Ministry and Health Ministry for partnership and financial help whenever I exhausted my travel funds.

I am grateful to 430 groups in the nation for inviting me as a speaker and 116 hosts including 95 families who welcomed me into their homes while I was traveling. My daring six-year experience was a wonderful learning opportunity.

I am grateful to many people who devote their lives to the mission of bringing many homeless Americans home. I grew, matured, and humbled through meeting them, visiting many wonderful homeless programs and hearing many moving stories. Therefore, I am compelled to share them by formulating this final reflection as my gift to those who supported me to carry out this mission.

Reflecting upon the ministry with homeless women in Seattle and speaking to Presbyterians to end homelessness all meant "planting the cross," as God commanded me to do in my dream in 1988; planting motivation, the original image of woman God created, dignity, self-esteem, and hope, love, and the forgiveness of Jesus Christ in the souls of homeless women and planting the value, life and commandment of Jesus Christ to love "the least of these" in the hearts of the Presbyterians. We all are called to plant the cross, Jesus Christ, in everyone's soul and life. It was also marching on with God, Jesus and the purple people.

This writing goes beyond reporting and reflecting my journey with the homeless initiative. I share resources as well for those who seek new ideas. I have many stories to tell and it was hard to restrain myself from writing so much. Details may be found in the "Jubilee Manual" and five volumes at jeankimhome.com. Shalom to all who are involved in the mission of ending homelessness! Let's keep on marching!

CHAPTER 30

Marching to Seminary

I was seventy years old. My husband had saved up $10,000 to buy a car but his doctor told him he couldn't drive anymore due to his full-blown diabetes. He told me if I worked on a doctoral degree he would give me that money. So I said, "Okay, I will do it." That's how I marched to San Francisco Theological Seminary to be enrolled in the doctor of ministry program.

The first year, I drove from Seattle to San Francisco. It took me two full days. I worked laboriously on the theme, "Root Causes of the Homelessness in the U.S. and the Church's Response." I had great fun writing this dissertation. Many people seemed to have enrolled in the classes for a degree per se, but at my age I didn't need another degree. I wanted to write a good resource book for the church. I read through hundreds of resources, which was unnecessary for the D. Min course. But I wanted to update my knowledge on sociology, economy, culture, and theology. I had great fun being exposed to these resources.

In my second year, I fell in our condo parking lot, and broke my ankle. So I flew this time to SFTS with a cast on my leg. I couldn't sit on the chair too long, so I used to sit on the floor of my classroom, leaning my back to the wall and the laptop on my lap. That's how I wrote my papers until my ankle healed. It was difficult, but joyful and I was grateful for the opportunity. I know I made it through since God marched with me.

My deathly-ill husband also marched with me; I carried my laptop wherever he was taken to the emergency room, intensive care, progressive care, dialysis center, and his nursing home. Kept on marching with writing my dissertation—until his last breath.

My whole family, my son, daughter-in-law, and the three grandchildren came to my graduation at the San Francisco Theological Seminary. I wanted them to witness that regardless of one's age, one can pursue any

level of education if one so desires. God and good people will march with you. My husband, too, marched with me. I was seventy-one when I got my doctor of ministry degree. I was very glad that I did it.

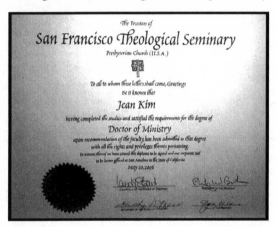

CHAPTER 31

Marching Nest Mission

After serving on a national Network to End Homelessness, I kept organizing a local mission within the church community to end homelessness. In 2006, I developed the Nest Mission in Lynnwood, WA. It was, in fact, conceived this way: I met Yoo Bok Nim, a D. Min student at San Francisco Theological Seminary in 2004 while I was doing my work on my doctor of ministry degree. I invited her to develop a homeless mission in Lynnwood, Washington, where I was and am still residing. She came and stayed with me while she tried to develop one in Tacoma, Washington. Things didn't work out and she went back to San Francisco, after which Rev. Min Kwon Ok and Kyung Ho Lee and I met discussed to develop one in the Lynnwood area, where I will be working closely without driving long distance. I laid out the purpose from the onset to be "ending homelessness." First, I suggested to call it Washington State Korean American Coalition for the Homeless to include as many Korean American Churches as possible as a coalition. I designed the purpose of the mission as follows:

1. To put into action the compassion of Jesus Christ for the homeless
2. To help end homelessness
3. To urge and challenge Korean-American immigrant community to share their blessings with the local poor
4. To guide the homeless to God, that they may find hope and be motivated to live as responsible and productive citizens
5. To help experience holistic salvation by meeting physical, emotional, and spiritual needs

We have been operating this mission entirely with volunteers, and all funds are being used to support people in need.

Since I hold licenses in social work and mental health, I took charge of the case manager's responsibility. And I was a retired person and also took on full administrative duty in the beginning until we secured enough volunteers. I went on to apply to IRS for non-profit 501(C)(3) tax-exemption status. Most of the mission identity and program came out of my own experience. I was the sole runner in the beginning. Thus, my colleagues honored me with the title "founder of the Nest Mission."

Later, I suggested to change the name to the Nest Mission, Matthew 8:20, where I got the "nest" concept from Jesus's claim that he didn't have anywhere to lay his head while the birds in the air have a nest. Our major mission was to help find a "nest" for the homeless and help them move in. I invited people to serve on the board and as volunteers. Therefore, the first board was made up mainly of my hand-picked folks. In the beginning, we didn't have much funding. Rev. and Mrs. D.S. Jung chipped in with their tithes. We owe them a huge gratitude for this.

After that I developed the details of the mission, which included worship, soliciting local support from Korean congregations by doing outreach, and gathering homeless friends by visiting them where they hung out. I then informed social service agencies to take advantage of our resources to help homeless people to settle in apartments. We then began to pay for moving expenses such as deposit and/or first month's rent. A couple of years later, we added worship and dinner and distribution of daily necessities at the dinner. I solicited local church groups to cook by visiting each one individually.

Who Do We Serve?

With limited resources, our priority for service goes to the homeless or needy neighbors who are in crises, referred by members of area churches, many of whom were formerly homeless. We don't see Korean homeless. The homeless population includes those who are laid off or evicted from their homes due to the economic downturn. Some are victims of abuse and broken homes, chronic substance abuse, domestic violence, divorce, and emotional issues. Many haven't had good role models and suffer from poor life skills. Some are employable but can't find work. Many lost hope and motivation. The need is great. Being fed is just a basic necessity. We are called to serve beyond feeding toward healing and self-sufficient life. So the Nest Mission started to march with homeless friends.

Who Supports Us?

Up to now, the major financial supporters are Korean immigrants with occasional support from the English-speaking community. The size of monetary contributions ranges from $10 to $2,000 at a time. Some support us with in-kind donations. We have many angels who are willing to share their blessings with the local homeless. We thank God for them. Praise the Lord!

Who Are Our Mission Partners?

For Friday evening dinner we partner with Maplewood Presbyterian Church with a free site in Edmonds and a monthly dinner. The rest of the dinners are offered by Korean immigrants. We have a few English-speaking friends in these groups. We partner with other churches for emergency assistance, labor works, Christmas gifts of motel rooms, etc. Without a partnership, this mission is impossible! Together with God marching with us, we see some miracles.

Guidelines for Rental Assistance:

Persons or families that need rental assistance must be homeless in the state of Washington. We will request the shelter counselors to apply for assistance on behalf of their client(s). We will rely on the client's case workers to assess the needs and follow up with the client afterward.

1. A client must have found an apartment and be ready to move in but needs assistance with first month rent and/or deposit.
2. A client must expect some income to afford the rent after moving in. We won't be able to offer rental assistance more than once. The amount of rental assistance will vary depending on each situation.
3. A client must receive an ongoing support service from an agency.
4. We will not discriminate against clients based on gender, sexual orientation, nationality, religion, or legal status.
5. In order to expedite the process, we want to receive the application electronically. We will respond or issue a check within a week on a first-come, first-served basis.
6. No phone requests. No direct phone calls from clients.

Emergency Respite Beds at Motels

For the sick homeless individuals or families with young children that are evicted with no place to go we give priority to motel beds. It is short-term but life-saving for them to have a temporary place to stay warm and dry until they find a better place to move to.

Healing Weekly Dinner

We offer a balanced hot dinner cooked with fresh groceries. This meal is a good tonic for the sick, strength for the elderly, welcome for the alienated, love for the deserted, hope for the discouraged, joy for the depressed, a community for the lonely. It is a place to meet God through singing, worship, message, prayers, and people. We cook a fancy dinner as if we have Jesus himself at our table (Matthew 25: 40). It is a communion with Jesus. Therefore, we sing a communion song before each meal. We are mindful of those who have health problems or are vegetarians for religious reasons.

Men, women, children, and whole families enjoy dinner every Friday evening.

Offer of Daily Supplies

After each Friday dinner we offer items such as bus tickets, socks, razors, underwear, clothes, soap, shampoo, lotion, toothbrushes, toothpaste, batteries, toilet papers, ramen, etc.

Worship

1. Spirituality for homeless people is very important as they often ask serious spiritual questions as to who they are, what is the purpose of their life, and where God is in all their struggles.
2. Many dinner guests express their need to cry out to God for help.
3. The Board of the Nest Mission as well as the Korean cooking groups want to offer our dinner guests a chance to worship God as our purpose

states, but we don't impose Christian faith on them. We respect their choices. We encourage them to come in, sit in the back, and pray to their own God if they are not interested in our Christian God.

4. The worship service and the messages help undo the damage done to them by helping them experience a positive, loving, and forgiving God rather than a judging, condemning God.

5. They are encouraged to lay down all their troubles and guilt before God and experience healing.

Singing/Choir

Most homeless people are victims of physical, emotional, and sexual violence, many of whom carry unresolved wounds. Thus, they sing out all their pains, problems, grief, anger, and hatred. Singing is spiritual as well as therapeutic. We have a choir that makes a joyful noise to God. A few local church choir members participate to support them. I brought my experience of singing at the homeless women's church, Seattle, downtown to the Nest Mission. I discovered that women singers are livelier and tend to express their emotion more openly than men. We have more men at the Nest Mission worship.

Weekly Bible Study

We did Bible study at the library, at a park in summer or a Subway sandwich shop. It serves a group therapy session for the participants as they apply the Bible messages to their troubled life. gave each Bible class member nice small Bible that they should  carry in their backpack and remember they are carrying the words of God as if God was with them always. One day, while we were waiting for a bus, one member pulled out his Bible and began to read it. It was such a sacred moment for this man to be engaged in the words of God.

Christmas Gift of Rooms

I know from my experience Christmas is the loneliest time for homeless friends. Few of them have a family to go to or are invited by anyone.

To remember the baby Jesus born homeless in a manger and to

provide warm beds we offer **gift of motel rooms** for two or three nights beginning from Christmas Eve with clean underwear, a gift package, and meals. So we claim, *"There will be a room at the inn tonight."* Since Christmas 2011 the Korean Community Church

has partnered with us and made the gift of three nights possible. Praise the Lord!! This church thus has been running the march with the Nest Mission. Crisis intervention, job search, summer retreat, laundry service, birthday celebration, certificate for community service have been added.

Retreat to Develop Leadership

In the first retreat, participants were highly motivated to start a choir and Bible study group.

They have been going for the past twelve years.

When the sun is very hot we all sit in this secluded and private space for serious discussion. Amazing results are being produced.

I have been marching with the Nest Mission and vice versa ever since, up to the date that I became disabled due to my spinal fracture.

CHAPTER 32

Marching with Awards

I am very embarrassed to have received twenty-four awards during my service. Whenever I was reluctant, my board usually encouraged me to go and receive them just to encourage others to serve the needy in our neighborhood and cities. I can't post all twenty-four here, but will introduce a few of them.

They might have praised my active role in developing Human rights and democracy movements in South Korea during the era of dictatorships. And they might have perceived service for the homeless as being their voices when they have no voices of their own.

Asian Pacific American Community Voice Award from the International Examiner Newspaper, May 26, 1993

Every award made me feel humble, thinking that I don't deserve such recognition.

My Medal of Honor signed by Dae Jung Kim, then President of Korea

I couldn't go to Korea and therefore, they brought it to the Koran Consulate in Seattle. Their meeting room was so small that I invited only a few people to represent different sectors in Seattle I worked very closely with. They were and still are important supporters of my homeless mission.

The late Rev. Dr. Bill Cate (far left in the front row) represented the interfaith and church community. Lori Matsukawa (third from the left, front row, King 5 anchorwoman) represented the media. Jan Cate (the fourth on the left in the front row) and the late Barbara Wilson (the fifth from the left on the front row) represented the women's community.

Rev. Boyd Stockdale (on the right far back row) represented Seattle Presbytery, and the rest united the different sectors of the Seattle community.

On the left is the Medal of Honor from the Korean Government for Social Service, Dec 31, 1998, Signed by President Kim, Dae Jung

Award from Ewah Girls' High School in Seoul, Korea

Ewah Girls' High School in Korea, my alma mater. Photo taken with my husband, and nieces residing in Korea.

May 31, 2000, I received awards for social service

The same day, I was invited to visit the First Lady of Korea at the Presidential Mansion, the Blue House.

With my husband at the entrance of the Blue House With the First Lady Lee Hee Ho in her office at the Blue House.

Woman of Faith Award by Presbyterian Church (U.S.A.)

Hero of the Homeless by the Night Watch. Me with Ron Sims, former King County Executive.

Woman of Hope Award

It is my honor to present the Woman of Hope Award. I could tell you about her many degrees of higher education, her extensive theological study, her profound social work, her eighteen-plus national and international awards, her continued participation in numerous boards since her retirement, or the abuse and trauma of her childhood within her family of origin as well as the Korean War. Instead let me share with you the relationship she has with her sisters at the Church of Mary Magdalene and my experience of this person. She is a fiery, energetic, hardworking, "no challenge is too big" DYNAMO!

She has stood beside the homeless women and children on the streets of Seattle telling them they are good, worthy, and lovable until they believed it themselves. She has scooped the sick, the hungry, the lonely, the depressed, the traumatized, and the abused off the streets into her van to comfort, to console, and give them the resources, help, love, and acceptance they needed most.

Her vision prompted by God has pushed her and all of us here to meet women and children at their need.

When I heard the story of the Church of Mary Magdalene coming out of her own healing process of the loss of her son, I was overwhelmed…as this is the most devastating loss any human being can suffer. She has experienced many losses, this to the greatest extent.

Her being open to the Holy Spirit's leading has set in motion this ministry to homeless women and children, which has grown to serving over 100 women and children per day, six days a week, to a jail ministry, a pen pal outreach, a hospital ministry, working relationships with over 200 churches, church women's groups in the Puget sound region, emergency shelter for homeless families, inspirational worship services and a faith filled, soul-filled homeless women's choir!

She gave birth to this mission over twenty years ago. She continues to support the church through her time, talent, treasure, wisdom, expertise and presence. She has seen us through some of our most difficult days by mobilizing churches and the community to advocate for a new home, for funding to make it happen and sharing prayer and encouragement for all of us. When we face challenges and seeming catastrophes, we are like children seeking their mother for help, encouragement and direction.

It is with great thankfulness and appreciation we present this award to our founding pastor, our mom, our sister, our friend . . . Rev. Jean Kim.

Executive Director
Church of Mary Magdalene / Mary's Place

CHAPTER 33

Marching Eightieth Birthday

Jean Kim Foundation for Homeless Education

As my eightieth birthday was approaching, my family wanted to celebrate it in a distinctive way. But, I had an idea to ask friends and relatives to not give me any birthday gifts, but to instead make contributions toward education funds for the homeless. Two hundred gracious friends and relatives came to celebrate the event and gave generous contributions, which gave birth to the Jean Kim Foundation for Homeless Education, a 501(C)(3) tax exempt, non-profit organization. In all my professional life of serving poor and homeless friends, I have carried this belief: *"Had they acquired college education and job skills, they wouldn't have had to depend on welfare and live a homeless life."* We are living in a day and age that will not allow us to survive if we don't get an education/job training with some skills. So I decided to make my eightieth birthday a march with my dear homeless friends. Part of this march was passing out copies of my autobiograhy (in Korean) and my CDs and DVDs about the "purple people." Read on to see what has been happening since then!

Celebrating my 80th birthday!

Mission Statement

The Foundation's goal is to break the chain of poverty through education by motivating homeless adults to pursue college education for the degrees, certificates, and vocational skills that are the essential tools to lead them to gainful employment and permanent housing. **To advocate to achieve the above goals** we uncover God-given hidden talents, potential, and possibilities in the homeless adult population, bring them out into the light, and guide and empower them through case management service, which includes active ongoing outreach, guiding them to obtain federal student aid, enrollment to colleges, crisis prevention, intervention, tangible aids/support, and engagement with community services. **Our mission is being carried out** in partnerships with citizens, colleges, local community groups/services, faith communities, and government entities to ensure these students' success. In a lay person's experience I understand our mission in the following medical terms:

The modern medical approach is, in a layperson's terms, mostly symptom control/reduction by chemical agents and/or by a surgical approach. However, many symptoms our students experience are not surgically correctable.

The herbal medicine approach is boosting or strengthening the positive potential patients might have. Strengthening their immune system allows patients to overcome the battle with their disease. This is the approach the JKF mission has taken. We seek out talent, potential, and possibilities in the adult homeless population, and guide and empower them through supportive services, which can be an extra tonic or nutrients to boost their already existing talent and potential. We also guide them to obtain federal student aid and walk with them through the enrollment process for colleges. After they start their classes, we provide ongoing outreach, crisis prevention, intervention, tangible aids/support, and engagement with community services to ensure their success and prevent drop outs.

Why Education?

Although most of us know the importance of education, here are a few eye-opening research results.

Peter Vander Weyst, a JKF board member and a faculty member of Edmonds Community College, helps potential homeless students to apply for federal student aid at Lynnwood Library.

The Link between Illiteracy, Poverty, and Homelessness

According to a study conducted by the U.S. Department of Education and the National Institute of Literacy, 32 million adults in the U.S. can't read, and 19 percent of high school graduates can't read. [16] Illiteracy and Poverty: 75 percent of Americans who receive food stamps perform at the lowest levels of literacy, and 90 percent of high school dropouts are on welfare.[17] Struggling readers from low-income families are 13 times less likely to complete high school than their peers who can read proficiently. Not graduating high school can put a damper on ambitious career plans and makes it that much harder to break out of the poverty level.[18]

Earnings and unemployment rates by educational attainment, 2015

	Median usual weekly earnings	Unemployment rate
Doctoral degree	$1,623	1.7%
Professional degree	$1,730	1.5%
Master's degree	$1,341	2.4%
Bachelor's degree	$1,137	2.8%
Associate's degree	$798	3.8%
Some college, no degree	$738	5.0%
High school diploma	$678	5.4%
Less than a high school diploma	$493	8.0%

All workers: $860   All workers: 4.3%

Note: Data are for persons age 25 and over. Earnings are for full-time wage and salary workers.
Source: U.S. Bureau of Labor Statistics, Current Population Survey

---

[16] DoSomething.org. 19 West 21st St, 8th Floor. New York, NY 10010 (Online source)

[17] Ibid.

[18] Seattle-King County Committee to End Homelessness.

Illiteracy and Health Care

Low literacy directly costs the health care industry over $70 million every year.[19] Health literacy is the "ability to read, understand, and act on health care information." [20] Fourteen percent of U.S. adults struggle to read medicine labels, maps, or names on a ballot. [21]

JKF board member and director of finance of Seattle Pacific University Ted Haase (center) helps potential homeless students to apply for federal student aid at Lynnwood Library.

Illiteracy and Homelessness

In America there are more than 550,000 families with young children who are homeless. These homeless children are at a higher risk for not becoming literate, simply because of their living conditions. In fact, children who have not been well-fed or well-nurtured, are less healthy and subsequently less ready to learn than their peers. The lack of a high school diploma is associated with homelessness for individuals and families. Therefore, poverty and illiteracy and lack of education and homelessness are all closely linked.[22] Nationally, a high proportion of homeless individuals are employed. Fifty percent of homeless adults have incomes of less than $300 per month. A lack of educational opportunities limits access to living-wage jobs.

Illiteracy and Crime Rates

According to the Department of Justice, "The link between academic failure and delinquency, violence, and crime is welded to reading failure." The stats back up this claim: two-thirds of students who cannot read

---

[19] DoSomething.org. 19 West 21st St, 8th Floor, New York, NY 10010.

[20] Ken Kraybill & Sharon Morrison. *Promoting Wellness.* Health Literacy 2011.

[21] CharitySub's Cause: THE LITERACY GAP, Mar 2012.

[22] Seattle-King County Committee to End Homelessness.

proficiently by the end of fourth grade will end up in jail or on welfare.[23] More than 60 percent of all prison inmates are functionally illiterate.[24] Eight-five percent of all juveniles who interface with the juvenile court system are functionally illiterate, and more than 70 percent of inmates in America's prisons cannot read above a fourth-grade level.[25]

Therefore, education with degrees, certifications, and vocational skills is the primary tool to end welfare, crime, and homelessness with earning power, living-wage full-time-employment, and permanent housing.[26]

Who We Serve

Most community college adult students are healthy and bright, but most of those I love and serve are high school dropouts or did some college work; they are physically and/or emotionally challenged with many barriers to employment, including financial troubles, rental barriers, and homelessness; carry past prison/jail experience, substance use, mental challenges (such as PTSD, bipolar disorder, depression, anxiety disorders, attention deficit disorder, paranoia from past abuse and trauma, personality issues). Most of them survive on food stamps and some do day labor work, which can never afford rent and living. Almost all of them want to work but cannot find jobs that can support them; some are on small disability checks but the above barriers prevent them from finding employment or housing.

However, despite these many obstacles, they hold God-given potential and possibilities. In this potential I try to plant a little seedling of motivation to pursue college education to build better careers to end their poverty and homelessness.

And I nurture that little fragile plant with love, care, nutrients, hope, and encouragement. I am thrilled to see more of those little plants survive.

---

[23] Begin To Read.com. Owned and managed by Write Express Corporation (Online source)

[24] DoSomething.org. 19 West 21st St, 8th Floor, New York, NY 10010 (Online source)

[25] BeginTo Read.com. Owned and managed by WriteExpress Corporation.

[26] www.huffingtonpost.com/2013/09/06/illiteracy-rate. (Online source)

Why People Are Homeless in the U.S.

Although it is a very complicated issue that includes personal, socio-political and cultural-economic aspects, on the surface homelessness often seems to stem from unemployment, underemployment, lack of education or job skills, accidents and injuries, poor health, as well as physical, emotional, or psychological disabilities, generational poverty, alcohol or drug addiction, eviction, and prior incarceration. These challenges often destroy peoples' hope and their motivation to try to improve their lives. The loss of hope pushes them into paralyzing despair, which creates a vicious cycle. Thus, they are often trapped in long-term unemployment and homelessness.

Some have enough earning to cover the rent from work and/or disability benefits, or couple together, but immediate visible causes appear to be:

1. **Lack of jobs for those with low-level education and lack of job skills** except labor works, which won't pay enough for anyone to afford rent and living.
2. **Lack of housing for those who can't afford unsubsidized rent.**
3. **Skyrocketing rent and high demands with deposit and first and last month's rent in advance** make it impossible for them to afford housing on top of all of the above obstacles.
4. **Disability checks are usually too small** to afford any housing at the current market rate.
5. **Too long waiting for subsidized low-income housing—five to ten years**—makes it impossible for them to rent housing, for which they pay one-third of their income and two-thirds is subsidized.
6. Often their physically and emotionally **challenging conditions are too heavy, and their health is not strong enough** to do labor work. Many who hold "homeless signs" on the streets look healthy but might belong to this invisible category. Let me add that our economic policy created poverty, which then created forty-three kinds of negative outcomes that all contribute to the above problems of homelessness.

45 Symptoms of Poverty

Personal Homelessness

Family Homelessness

Homelessness of Children

Youth Homelessness

Student Homelessness

Veteran Homelessness

Elderly Homelessness

Farm Worker Homelessness

Native American Homelessness

Ex-Prisoner Homelessness

Homelessness of the Mentally Ill

Homelessness of the Physically

Disabled

Domestic Violence

Substance Addiction

Divorce

Nuclear Family System

Tragedy

Post-Traumatic Stress Disorder

Minimum Wage

Gentrification

Foreclosure

Natural Disasters

Complex Building Codes

Illiteracy and Lack of Education

Bad Credit

Lack of Affordable Housing

Lack of Affordable Health Care

Lack of Child Support

Lack of Support System

Slashed Public Assistance

Tax Policy

Legal Issues

Racism

Criminal Justice System

Criminalization of the Homeless

NIMBY (Not-in-My-Backyard)

Syndrome

Human Rights Violation

Rural Homelessness

Tent Cities

Social/Cultural Values

Poverty—Feminization

Poverty

Lack of Political Will

U.S. Economic System/Policy

Where do all of these come from then? Besides individual issues such as growing up in generational poverty with lack of healthy parental care and role models and discipline in destructive home environments, there seems to be a larger picture

Looking at the root causes of homelessness in the U.S. from a sociopolitical, economic, and cultural standpoint, we find that our current economic system is chiefly responsible because it creates **unprecedented wealth and poverty and an ever-widening gap between the two with ever-growing income disparity.** While many Americans benefit from the current economic prosperity, **our economic system** has also created **poverty** and given birth to many negative outcomes (forty-three), such as lack of affordable housing, lack of jobs for all people who desire to work, ever-skyrocketing rent unaffordable to the poor, too many high rental barriers/restrictions, low minimum wage, gentrification, inadequate welfare, slashed public assistance, racism, unfair tax policies, social/cultural values (money and power devalue the poor and homeless), lack of long-term treatment services with vocational training and housing for substance users and the mentally challenged, or formerly incarcerated people, and a *lack of political will* to end poverty and homelessness in the United States. Most of the above are *policy issues.* However, our policy makers appear to be complacent. Very few presidential candidates mention the poor/homeless this country but rather talk about the middle class. This has created a society that throws 700,00 citizens, including students grade school to college age, into homelessness every night.

In their book *The Spirit Level: Why Greater Equality Makes Societies Stronger* Richard Wilkinson and Kate Pickett comment:

Global unemployment is now at its highest levels since the Great Depression. Rifkin (Biosphere Politics, LJ 5/15/91) argues that the Information Age is the third great Industrial Revolution. A consequence of these technological advances is the rapid decline in employment and purchasing power that could lead to a worldwide economic collapse. Rifkin foresees two possible outcomes: a near workerless world in which people are free, for the first time in history, to pursue a utopian life of leisure; or a world in which unemployment leads to an even further polarization of the economic classes and a decline in living conditions for millions of people. Rifkin presents a highly detailed analysis of the technological developments that have led to the current situation, as well as intriguing, yet alarming, theories of what is to come.

It is a remarkable paradox that, at the pinnacle of human material and technical achievement, we find ourselves anxiety-ridden, prone to depression...Driven to consume and with little or no community life. Lacking the relaxed social contact and emotional satisfaction we all need, we seek comfort in over-eating, obsessive shopping and spending, or become prey to excessive alcohol, psychoactive medicines and illegal drugs. *How is that we have created so much mental and emotional suffering despite levels of wealth and comfort unprecedented in human history?*

The common problems in unequal societies are related to level of trust, mental illness (including drugs and alcohol), life expectancy and infant mortality, obesity, children's educational performance, teenage pregnancy, homicide, imprisonment rates, social mobility. There is a very strong tendency for ill health and social problems to occur less frequently in the more equal countries.[27]

Could such analysis answer some questions as to why the campus shooting of our children has became a popular trend these days?

Marching with College Students by Providing Nine Different Ways of Support

1. Help students to obtain federal student aid and enroll in community colleges or four-year colleges, including online courses in a variety of subjects.
2. We work with current and potential students for job search – temporary jobs or internships or jobs related to the subjects of their study.
3. Vocational training in partnership with Apprenticeship programs, CATCH (health care career), and adult culinary arts (cooking). This job training will include pay, college credits, certification, and job placement.
4. If students do not want level one or level two, we can help them vocational skill training through the Department of Vocational Rehabilitation.
5. We can also offer an individualized literacy program; reading and writing.
6. We help those who are in trouble with the law to pursue college education in partnership with the Next Step Program of Edmonds Community College.
7. We offer temporary housing (tents) for single homeless students.
8. We offer case management service with tangible material aids according to needs.
9. We also do referral services.

---

[27] Ibid. (Richard Wilkinson & Kate Pickett. *The Spirit Level: Why Greater Equality Makes Societies Stronger* (NY: Bloomsbury Press, 2010)

Marching with Tents

We serve poor and homeless adults who want to pursue college degrees or job skill training. Among them are seniors, veterans, racial ethnic minorities, domestic violence survivors, immigrants, and trafficking survivors. They are economically impoverished Washington State residents. Most of them receive food stamps at $194 value per month, which qualifies them for federal student aid. Some live in low-income subsidized housing, but many are homeless and/or couch surfing, living

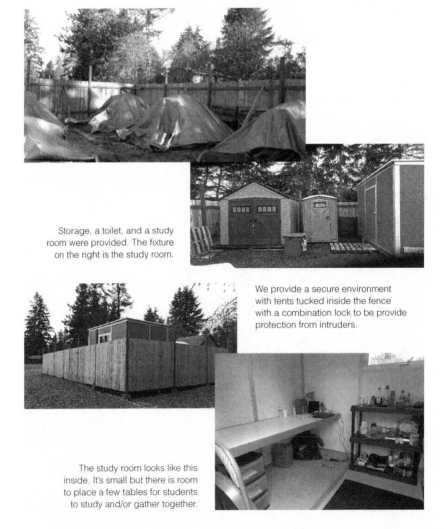

Storage, a toilet, and a study room were provided. The fixture on the right is the study room.

We provide a secure environment with tents tucked inside the fence with a combination lock to be provide protection from intruders.

The study room looks like this inside. It's small but there is room to place a few tables for students to study and/or gather together.

in cars or on the streets. Many struggle with multiple obstacles. We have discovered that, without stable housing, educational goals never can be achieved. Homelessness is the biggest barrier that causes students to drop out of colleges and every aspect of life.

The gracious approval from the City of Lynnwood and the Good Shepherd Baptist Church allowed us to start with five tents for five homeless Edmonds Community College students.

Rain and snow collapsed the tents in January and February and all through the rainy season, and tents became uninhabitable.

We installed a canopy over the tents which worked fine in the summer. During the winter of 2017 residents had to scrape the snow off the roof during the night to prevent the snow piling up and collapsing the canopy.

6 tiny houses are tucked inside the fence with a locked gate on the property of Good Shepherd Baptist Church in Lynnwood, WA.

Therefore, our final plan is to install tiny houses instead of tents. We hope to replace the tents with tiny houses before rain falls this year (2018). As I finish this writing, the six tiny homes are going up. Praise the lord!

Tiny House Ribbon Cutting Ceremony on Nov. 18, 2018

Marching with a Broken Spine

An angel invited me to California, where weather was warmer than Seattle, to finish up my writing. As soon as I landed at L.A. airport, my back pain started. When I got to the house in the evening the pain worsened. But I was able to fix my meal and walk a few hundred steps to the park. That evening I couldn't climb the stairs to go to bed in the upstairs bedroom. I ended up sleeping on the couch downstairs.

The second day was the same. The third day, symptoms of bronchitis were creeping in. I called Paul Han, my nephew, who came to get me at 10 p.m. By that time my symptoms had gotten worse. He took me to the UC Irvine Hospital emergency room. After I  was treated I moved down to Chan Hie Park's home in Orange County because her house is one story. While I stayed at her house for ten days, I had pain in my spine but was able to walk to the dining room and even take a short walk around her swimming pool—about 100 steps. But the day I was leaving for home (March 10, 2018) my back pain worsened. I had to lean on Paul a lot while I was checking in at the airport. By the time I landed in Seattle I couldn't walk. Sam, my son, literally carried me into his car and I had to lie down in the back seat while he drove me home.

Ever since, I have been bedridden with a walker to lean on to go about ten feet at the most.

X-rays and an MRI showed that I had a broken spine bone and two pinched nerves, which was the reason why I was having a double dose of pain. I could only take general pain pills, which are not as effective as narcotics but left me with a clear brain, which I preferred. The doctor suggested that I have surgery for pinched nerves but let my broken spine heal by itself.

In all of this I couldn't stop marching with my students who were experiencing crises because we didn't have a replacement for my position yet. I ended up inviting student interns to my condo to give them instructions how to start their internships. Tony and Donna have been extremely helpful for running chores for me, including contacting students.

Here are examples of crises:

One evening, a woman student was running into a crisis. She went to the U. District to give books back to the store that was buying back her used book to get a few dollars cash to get by until the next financial help kicked in. The staff at the college finance office went on vacation, leaving her in financial limbo. And the store, instead of buying her book back was closed by the time she got there, and she also ran out of gas. Her phone was going to cut off if she didn't pay the bill that evening. Her cell phone was dying and she had no gas to return to her home or to come to pick up the check from me. I couldn't say "I'm bedridden and can't do anything about this." Since it was Friday evening, I had to call the Nest Mission dinner site and arranged someone to take my check to Verizon. I called the phone company to let them know that someone is coming with my check. The staff knew me from past encounters with payment of other students' phone bills. And when I was just about to send my son down to her with gas, she called me weeping and reporting that she got around five dollars (no idea how, perhaps panhandling) and put a little gas in, just enough to go back home. A little while later she texted me that she got home safely.

One of my board members who stopped by to see me scolded me for doing all these in my pain. How can you stop marching just for your own needs to be met, leaving a student who is having a crisis out there on three street?

Another student called and reported his car had died on the street. It had been a few nights already and the car was going to be impounded by police any minute. He and his girlfriend had been sleeping in that car while they attended college. If it was impounded, their transportation would be gone. I had to call Tony to arrange towing. I instructed the student to contact the college's emergency fund, which could match our funds to fix his car. If that didn't work out I would have to raise funds through friends to cover the cost because it sounded like a big job repairing the car's transmission. Now, how can I say no to this crisis of imminent impounding of his car? Usually when this happens they lose their cars because they cannot afford the storage fee that grows on a daily basis. How can I say no when I have some resources and strategies? So I kept marching on with my students even with my broken back and bedridden situation.

My husband passed away in 2007, so I was living alone in my condo. The pain from my broken spine was unbearable. It was terribly devastating and discouraging. After two months I wasn't getting better, and walking was even more painful.

Fifteen warm-hearted, caring friends (along with my family members) came by to take me to doctor's appointments or to bring food and to help with chores. Two weeks after the pain started Evergreen Rehab sent a nurse, a physical and occupational therapist, and a shower helper once a week by doctor's order.

Some might say "you had plenty of helpers." Yes, I did. But I had many more hours alone in that condo. It was extremely difficult and painful to get out of bed and go to the bathroom leaning on the walker because the pain from my spine was shooting down my buttocks and legs and was so severe that I thought my left leg was fractured. I put so much pressure on my arms hanging onto the walker that both my arms and shoulders were in severe pain. I thought my shoulder was fractured too. But later I learned that spine pain is also connected to the shoulder nerves.

It was equally difficult to walk to the kitchen to eat food or drink water that friends got ready on the stove. Moving food from the stove to the dinning table—about a three-feet distance—was extremely difficult with one hand holding the walker and the other hand carrying food to the table. It was a very dangerous situation. Once I fell in my bathroom and couldn't get up. I couldn't think of any friends in my neighborhood, although there were a couple of them. My family was a good distance away. I didn't want to call 911. Finally, after a struggle, I managed to get up by holding onto the toilet. My tailbone was painful and I thought I had fractured it. An X-ray was taken and I found out it wasn't.

I was most fortunate to have that many friends to come by to help me, and I will be forever grateful to them. However, marching with a broken spine has been the most difficult, most painful and most lonely time in my whole life.

CHAPTER 35

Marching into Assisted Living

Because my situation didn't seem to be improving, family and friends helped me to choose assisted living as the best option for me. To make a long story short, we chose Brookdale Arbor Place. We visited the facility. There was a vacant studio apartment available. I quickly decided to take it, and moved in within two weeks. By this time the pain had become too unbearable for me to care what I owned. I was ready to give up most of my belongings, including my life if God wanted to take it. Since God didn't seem ready to take my life yet, I quickly moved

Assisted Living Facility: Brookdale Arbor Place.
12806 Bothell Everett Highway, Everett, WA 98208

with a small number of things I needed that could fill up the studio apartment. With such pain, God seemed to be training me to disown most of my possessions. I used to say that half of what we own belongs to someone else. Brueggemann wrote that justice is returning what belong to others. This was the time I practiced what I used to preach. Two thirds of what I owned was given to people. My son did a one-day moving sale but gave most of it away. This raised two questions. One was: How in the world can one person accumulate that much junk?! The second was: How in the world can one person disturb the whole community and receive such an overwhelming response from fifteen people who were physically present and hundreds of cards, e-mails, texts, and phone calls from others in the U.S. as well as Korea?!

Marching through Despair and Gratitude

My apartment is on the third floor, facing south, which means it gets plenty of sunlight with a view of lots of trees. I walk 100 steps to the elevator and 20 more from the elevator to my dining table. In pain, I need to walk this distance with walker and became manageable and even got used to it. I got acquainted with 3 other women at my table. I got to know many other residents. I have memorized the names of many servers and staff. I feel grateful to be at such a caring place and am trying to adjust to my new life. I'm not lonely anymore. There are staff, helpers, and many people, so I'm not alone all the time. However, the pain persists. About a month after my move I began to feel better and my pain was more manageable. But soon after that I discovered I had another spine fracture. Now the pain is back. No matter what I do—physical therapy and acupuncture—the pain is unbearable. Sometimes I envy those who are gone ahead of me. People might ask, where is your faith in God?

A Conversation with God

Dear God,

Of course, I am grateful to have you in my life. Of course, I have read the whole Bible in two months while I was struggling with pain. Of course, I am praying to you. Of course, I owe a huge gratitude to those who pray for me. Yes, faith is there. But every day, every hour I dance between gratitude and despair. It is a terrible place to be. But, God, you didn't seem to take the pain away. I begin to ask you, God, out of desperate frustration:

God, are you punishing me for my sins? No, you wouldn't punish me because you have already forgiven all my sins. You wouldn't punish me **with** such harsh brutal pain. You are a loving God and you would rather cry with me, participating in my pain. You still carry me on your back. I know you would feel sorry for me. You might be crying for me and with me. It is "me" who brought on this pain for not caring for myself. I lived and worked in the distorted belief that I was still a spring chicken. I forgot my age a long time ago. I didn't listen to the outcry of my body to stop abusing it with too many long hours of work. It is all my fault that I suffer like this. I knew someday I could drop dead from severe fatigue, which I preferred, but not such long-term painful dragging. But can't you, God, do something for this pain? Would you say the same thing you said to Paul, "The grace you got from me is sufficient" when Paul asked you take the **thorn** away from him? Yes, I know I got more than enough grace and blessings from you. I don't have the nerve to ask you to take this pain away. But, God, I cannot take it any longer. When is the end of my life coming? You might say, "It's not for you to know." But God, I envy those who are gone for good.

Now, I have my third broken spine bone in four months. It happened all by itself without a fall. When will the fourth or fifth broken bone come? Do you want me to live and suffer like this for more years? It will be too brutal. The doctor says the only solution is surgery. What if more broken bones come after surgery? Question after question comes up. Is this a sign of having no faith in you? When is the end of my life? Only you know. God, I just had a Reclast injection, which is treatment for osteoporosis, and I experienced five different side effects within five days.

Dear God, this morning, I woke up at 3:30 and prayed in bed asking God, "What is your will for me?" I was thinking of scheduling a surgery toward the end of September because by that time I can complete some of the tasks I need to get out of the way. This surgery will determine whether I wake up with corrected a spine or not wake up for good. It suddenly dawned on me that one of my ongoing chronic health issues can suddenly flare up and can take my life away—they are lung fibrosis, chronic bronchitis, kidney issues, and precancerous esophagus—either during surgery or even before surgery or afterward. Yes, God, when this happens that can be my time go to. I wish they come before I suffer too much more from my broken spine. It certainly can come sooner and then I don't have to live with this painful broken spine for years to come. When my prayers and thoughts reached this point, dear God, I found peace in my mind, even joy. Could this be an answer to my prayer? With this peace in mind I plan to have a surgery October 10. I want to have it done before winter comes.

Marching Final Retirement

Jean Kim Foundation for Ending Homelessness through Education
PO Box 1835, Lynnwood, Washington 98046
Website: www.jeankimfoundation.org

I sent out the following personal note to all my supporters.
Personal Greeting from Jean Kim to Supporters
> **Save the Date and Plan to Come:**
> **Saturday, September 8, 2018, 6–8 p.m.**
> **For the Celebration of the Third Anniversary and Program**
> **of Jean Kim Foundation for the Homeless at Korean United**
> **Presbyterian Church with a free dinner**
> 8506 238th St. S.W. Edmonds, Washington 98026
> Two blocks west of Highway 99 on 238th Street.

> **Emcee: Jules Butler, new president of the JKF board**
> **Entertainment**: Total Experience Gospel Choir (Rev. Dr. Pat
> Wright) will shake your soul.
> **Speakers**: Marilyn Chase (Washington state senator), Jorge De
> La Torre (dean, Edmonds Community College) and homeless
> students.
> **Benediction**: Rev. Julie Josund, senior pastor of Edmonds
> Lutheran Church

I am debilitated: Some of you might have heard that since March 2018,
I was suddenly knocked down to bed for the last six months with three
fractures and two pinched nerves in my spine, without a fall. It is like
the sudden confinement of a vigorously flying bird in a cage by breaking

its wings. In short, I am paying a huge price for not taking care of my osteoporosis and vitamin D and calcium deficiency to run around for our mission, in the distorted belief that I was still a young chicken. There isn't much doctors can do except an unpromising surgery. It is discouraging and making me dance between despair and yet gratefulness for having God and all of you on my side. Thanks for your prayers, cards, and words of encouragement. Since I cannot take care of myself I have moved to an assisted living facility: Brookdale Arbor Place, 12806 Bothell Everett Hwy #311, Everett, Washington 98208.

I am retiring: While I am learning the hard way to lay my vigorous ambitions and responsibilities down I am retiring and am honored as a founder/president emeritus. I will assist and support the mission any way I can, including resourcing, mentoring, and fund-raising so that this viable and much needed mission can continue to bring as many homeless and poor people to colleges and/or job training, which can eventually lead to ending their poverty and homelessness.

The new leadership: The new president of the board is Mr. Jules Butler, who practices family law in the Lynnwood area. We also hired **a student coordinator, Jason Dunbar,** to carry on the mission after me. He was an unordained minister for twenty years of youth ministry and five years of homeless shower mission. Both men are highly committed to our mission goal to end poverty and homelessness through college education. I am introducing them to you hoping that you will love and support them as you have done with me. Both men, along with the rest of wonderful board, will do a superb job in carrying on this mission with your strong support.

I plan to attend our September 8 event with you all even in my wheel chair. I hope to see you all there. This will be my final retirement. Please come to march with me.

May God bless you.

With love and gratitude,
Jean Kim

CHAPTER 37

Marching to
the Operating Table

In the past, I have had thirteen surgeries, small and large, from sinus to hysterectomy to total knee replacement. But I didn't experience emotional and spiritual struggle like I have this time. I just blindly trusted the medical team, checked into the hospital, sometimes alone, left my car keys at the registration desk and got on the operating table after giving my last prayer. I came out of it all without any problem. But why am I agonized and distressed over the open-spine surgery this time? Do I have less faith than before? No way! I am a little more apprehensive this time due to my age, and existing health issues. I am not afraid of death, but I am afraid of pain and the potentially crippling outcome of surgeries. That makes me anxious and distressed.

I have been suffering for 7 months from 3 spontaneous fractures and 2 compression of my spine bones. 1 of 3 fractures is being healed and 2 to go. I must spend lots of time in bed. The longer I sit up in a chair, the more pain I suffer. The more I walk, the more I suffer. I can't take painkillers because they have too many side effects and make me more dysfunctional. This has been on-going for over six months. I tried several conventional treatments for compression: steroid injections, acupunctures, physical therapy and osteoporosis treatment (injection), all with no avail. The entire time I was bed-ridden except for trips to bathroom leaning on a walker. I couldn't bear any longer the torturous nerve pain that was shooting down from the compressed spine nerves through my back, buttock, groin, legs and toes. Consultations with orthopedic doctors revealed that three fractured spine bones can be healed over time. But two compressed/pinched nerves can only be healed with surgery.

As my last resort, I reluctantly decided to take a chance with surgery. I held no confidence of coming back to life because of my age, the statistical likelihood of not recovering from surgery and my other existing medical issues.

There are a couple of ways to deal with the surgical process. One is called "cementing" (lumbar spine vertebroplasty) and the other is open-spine surgery (laminectomy and medial facetectomy). The first is simpler than the latter. Both doctors claim their approach will bring a better outcome. I chose to go with the latter, believing that it's better to get to the root of problems, see them and do something about them. The operation was October 10, 2018 and I trusted whatever God was going to do with my life. I committed my life entirely into God's hands and feel blessed that She still has a purpose for me.

However, before going to the operating table, I must confess and be forgiven for all the unintentional sins I committed, and all the unintentional mistakes, wrong words and behaviors I exercised to my family and friends. And, may my Mother God burn all my sins into ashes, She may also burn the source of my pain in the spine by Her Fire and wash it away by her powerful Water Fall and raise me up as repaired and born-again person.

So, I would say, if She wakes me up on the other side, I will be grateful for no more pain, anguish, and everlasting heartaches and join all my loved ones in the Eternal God's Home whom I have missed so much. It will be my happiest day. My entire family and all my friends will come together to my memorial service singing "O Happy Day" for me and let my body be useful for others' benefit, whatever that may be.

But if I wake up on this side of life, I will be equally grateful that God may be allowing me to finish a few incomplete tasks or may open an entirely new horizon. The only choice I will have is to follow Her way. I want to have Her name be honored. I feel pain when I hear people blame her for not rescuing me from the pain. If she wants to rescue me, it is for her own sake, not to benefit me. I don't deserve any more blessings from Her. I want to hear people say "there is God alive and present in all our suffering. We trust Her, and She will carry us on her back. Her back is like our mother's tender back that comforts us, carries us and takes away all our pain. Praise be to Her name!!

As my last prayer I reached for Job's Prayer. "Naked I come from my mother's womb, and naked I shall return there; the Lord gave, and the Lord has taken away; blessed be the name of the Lord. I say, 'Everything will be done in Your will.' Now I surrender and commit my whole self— my body and soul—to Her completely and march onto the operating table in an absolute and perfect peace. Your will be done. Only Your name be honored! Amen!

So, readers might wonder what happened on or after the operating table. As the anesthesiologist put the mask on my mouth, I immediately experience shortness of breath. I wished I could take off the mask with my hand, but I decided to bear with it to be anesthetized. A few seconds later I was no longer conscious. Later, when I asked my son why I had a tube in my throat and my tongue was covered with blisters that hurt so bad to swallow after the surgery. He reported that I had difficulty breathing and a tube was inserted into my throat, perhaps to connect to a breathing machine. And during or after the surgery, my blood pressure went up so high that extra medication had to be administered. They kept me an extra two hours after surgery in the post-op-room before they brought me to the recovery room. Later, Doctor said this was all normal procedure.

The surgery was a risky one as I anticipated. However, God intervened and blessed Dr. Ali Anissipour, the surgeon, and to my surprise, God brought me back to life. The surgery stopped the torturous nerve pains in both legs. There remains pain from previous fractures and the surgery which is expected and manageable, but it doesn't radiate down my leg and will healed in time. The doctor promised 75% success from this surgery, but I am reporting 95% success. The fractured bones seem to be healing nicely. It was all God's doing. It is another one of God's story.

I invite all readers to join me and the surgeon to acknowledge that God was actively at work during my surgery. Thanks be to God and rejoice with me. But I will not be able to come back to my previous work. As a founder of the mission, I am willing to help in any way I can. Now, God must reveal Her will and plan for the remainder of my life. I will live and work only for Her honor. May God bless all my readers! Amen!

CHAPTER 38

I Want To Die This Way

Marching in with Singing

As I am aging, I often get to see friends leaving this world. I happened to be at their death beds. While I was watching them fight for life, I was thinking, "Why not fill the anxious and urgent last moments with spiritual songs instead of helplessly watching a painfully dying friend?" Then, it might become a comfort for those who are leaving and family and friends who are sending a friend off.

If I am blessed with sudden death, that will be wonderful. But if I have time, days, months at home or in a hospital setting, I hope people will fill that void with spiritual songs. I am not a singer but will enjoy listening at the last moments, which will become a comfort and will make me happy. Those songs we used to sing a lot at our services—either at Korean Churches or worship with our marching friends.

I prefer that my memorial service have no funeral songs. Because it is not a sad funeral but a happy day. We used to sing the following songs a lot: "Amazing Grace," "Precious Lord, Take My Hand," "Here I Am, Lord. Is it I, Lord?, "This Little Light of Mine," "When the Poor One Who Has Nothing," "We Shall Overcome," and "We Are Marching," etc.

And I wish my memorial service will become a songfest by family, friends and the Nest Mission choir, the Mary Magdalene choir, the Total Experience Gospel Choir, and many homeless students and friends. I asked Rev. Pat Wright to lead these choirs and participants to sing "O Happy Day." She and her choir sang this song at the memorial service for Rev. Bill Cate. That was a wonderful songfest. I want the same song and to make the whole event a happy day because it will be a happy day for me.

Marching in with No Flowers

I want a memorial service with no flowers. Yes, I used to like flowers very much. They used to offer me lots of wordless joy and comfort. My mother and I loved flowers. I used to hang three to four hanging flower baskets on my condo patio (as the photo shows). I enjoyed their blooms throughout the whole summer till the fall frost. I used to water them and talk to them. They were my friends.

I even used to raise African violets and orchids on the window sills by my dining room. They did the same thing as my hanging baskets.

So why am I requesting my memorial service with no flowers? Because I can't enjoy any of them, nor can I take some of them with me. Even if you cover my grave with them, they will be a total waste! I don't want to waste the love of my friends expressed in flowers. Thus, in lieu of flowers, friends may give something for our causes. I developed quite a few missions, Contributions will be split by some homeless missions that I had founded over the years and are still serving the homeless well. This contribution will be my last gift on earth for them hoping they continue to serve the most needy in our society whom I used to love and served. Guests might like this idea, too, instead of seeing their flowers turn into trash.

Marching in the Color Purple

By now, everyone knows purple is my color. The reason has been described at the beginning of this book. Those who feel like they are missing something without flowers can bring a cheap balloon. So no flowers, but the hall can be filled with cheap purple balloons. My soul will be more pleased with that than an expensive glamorous flower. And those who have purple clothes or ties may wear them too. That will be the best way to celebrate who I was in this world. My immediate family members, relatives, and homeless friends who have purple shirts may wear those also. There won't be any other more meaningful way to celebrate my life than these gestures. I call this "marching in the color purple."

Marching in with No "Body"

I thought about donating my body for quite some time. Cremation will waste the entire body and it will be costly too. But donating my body, organs, or parts of my body can be used for good purposes—scientific study and/or for research or to help medical students learn about the human body and diseases.

When I buried my dear son, Hyoung, I promised that I would lie next to him for good. This promise was made forty years ago, which I am breaking now. In a way I am guilty for doing this but, lying next to his bones six feet under might not mean anything to his soul. His and my soul wouldn't be sad to break this promise for a good purpose. The expense for funeral and burial service can be used for good causes. My soul and Hyoung's would rather be happy about this decision. I gather that my second living son, Sam, seems to have no reservation but is satisfied with my decision. I thank him for his understanding and acceptance of my decision. Thanks be to God for allowing me to share my nearly entire life with the homeless mission, which includes giving away my body for a good cause. But first I have to see if my old body is acceptable for the above purposes. I am registered for the donation of my body to the University of Washington medical school.

Epilogue: Final Reflection

I am very glad and overwhelmed to finish writing the rough draft of my story weaving it in with the story of my dear homeless friends.

The eighty-three years of my life have been spread around North Korea, South Korea, and the United States in Chon Shin Man Ko fashion. While I was writing out this life I traveled eighty-three years of life in the short span of a month, which was also an amazing experience.

I felt this length of years as ten thousand miles long. With lack of time, I pushed myself to travel through super quickly. Fortunately, events, memories, and feelings were neatly organized and stored in my brain, which was another amazing experience. Therefore, it wasn't hard at all to bring them out into the open, although many memories contained traces of pain. Some of them were buried and hidden in deeper storage than others. When fully exposed they made me weep a lot again.

First, I traveled to North Korea, where I lived for eleven years. I visited Ham Heung, Sun Duck, Sapori, and Hwang Keum Jung, but there weren't many good memories there, just the experience of sharing my mother's tears and the way my father abused her, which was stored there as clear and as ever.

Despite all that, the beautiful environment of Sun Duck village and three orchards remained as good, pleasant, and happy memories. There was also a memory of the whole nation's sadness of the 1930s and 1940s in being invaded, taken over, and occupied by Japan for too many years (thirty-six), which threw us into economic, political, and emotional poverty.

I was able to travel through the 1940s up to the 1960s. I remember the darkest time through the Korean War, which threw us into hunger, homelessness, and grief. Not only our beautiful country herself became desolate but our hearts and souls too were dried out like a desert. In the 1960s I remembered another level of suffering in the aftermath of the war, which left all of us desolate. Throughout these years my life was full of tears in despair as bad as the time of the war fighting through Chon Shin Man Ko.

However, life can't be all bad all the time. A door was open for me to enter junior and senior high at a Christians mission school, where I tasted the most valuable experience, which was meeting Jesus. I marched on to another college and seminary, married, and children came along. Life weaved fiercely between the hope and despair, along with the most rewarding, bright, and hopeful experience of passing the test for students going abroad and getting on the plane for the University of Chicago.

I also visited Bal Um, a muddy pit in the Kimpo area, where we lived prior to my departure for the Unites States for good. There were many painful memories of leaving my children with a babysitter and not being able to provide abundance for them at all. This is the most painful unforgettable memory that will never go away and is still overflowing with the river of my guilt. I have no idea when this river of guilt will dry out.

However, again, not everything was bad, and there were some good memories too. The sunshine of helping leper colonies and building churches penetrated my frozen, guilt-ridden heart and began to melt the ice a little. The biggest event was the direct intervention of God to rescue me out of the muddy pit. Therefore, I dare say that the twenty-four years of my life in South Korea were God's marching with me by carrying me on her back.

I look at my life in the Unites States. I have lived in St. Louis, Missouri, and Seattle, Washington. My life was colorful with many events happening, all mixed with joy and despair. The worst experience was and still is being left with an ever-grieving and ever-broken heart and ever-stained guilt. Through such suffering I achieved a lot, including career building and academic success. I wrote several books as an amateur writer. I received twenty-four undeserved awards for community service. I got to be ordained and carried out several homeless missions. I also gained as many brothers, sisters, friends, and children as the sands in the ocean and stars in the heaven. However, the bombshells that struck deep in my heart haven't gone away and keep hurting. I might have to march with them up to my last day. All that happened, including the bombshells, could have been God's blessings showered upon me. My life is a confession of such rich blessings and it is therefore, God's story. When there are many events that are beyond human imagination and explanation, the only word that is possible to describe it is "God."

I have no other way to describe it except to say that my half a century of life in the Unites States has been led by the Spirit of God. Therefore, my life is the testimony of her work as she carried me on her back. She was the One who helped me fight the good fight all along. Therefore, my eighty-three years of life is the proof that one of my hands holds all my illness and the other holds her hands and those of my homeless friends. She led me to education and service to my homeless friends. They might appear to be my work but no way that is true at all. Behind me there has been the Holy Spirit and my homeless friends who all have been marching with me. Therefore, this story of mine is God's and a testimony of that story.

Thanks be to God for creating human beings with everlasting and inerasable power of memory that can overcome the passage of time. I am loudly affirming, praise and honor God's power of creation. Psalmist (139) expressed this aspect so well:

Chapter 139 (NIV)
1. O Lord, you have searched me and known me. 2. You know when I sit down and when I rise up; you discern my thoughts from far away. 3. You search out my path and my lying down and are acquainted with all my ways. 4. Even before a word is on my tongue, O Lord, you know it completely. 5. You hem me in, behind and before, and lay your hand upon me. 6. Such knowledge is too wonderful for me; it is so high that I cannot attain it. 7. Where can I go from your spirit? Or where can I flee from your presence? 8. If I ascend to heaven, you are there; if I make my bed in Sheol, you are there. 9. If I take the wings of the morning and settle at the farthest limits of the sea, 10. even there your hand shall lead me, and your right hand shall hold me fast. 11. If I say, 'Surely the darkness shall cover me, and the light around me become night,' 12. even the darkness is not dark to you; the night is as bright as the day, for darkness is as light to you. 13. For it was you who formed my inward parts; you knit me together in my mother's womb. 14. I praise you, for I am fearfully and wonderfully made. Wonderful are your works; that I know very well. 15. My frame was not hidden

from you, when I was being made in secret, intricately woven in the depths of the earth. 16. Your eyes beheld my unformed substance. In your book were written all the days that were formed for me, when none of them as yet existed. 17. How weighty to me are your thoughts, O God! How vast is the sum of them! 18. I try to count them—they are more than the sand; I come to the end*—I am still with you.

God's Amazing Training and Discipling

Reflecting upon my past experiences, I confess that my life journey was in God's mysterious planning: First, in 1980, I was hired by Harborview Community Mental Health Center's in-patient unit where each of us—social worker or nurse—was assigned to treat two to three severe patients.

A year after, I was transferred to Intensive Community Support Treatment, which was a pioneer outpatient case-management program for the chronically mentally ill and most non-compliant patients in the same community. We had six teams of psychiatric nurses and social workers at the master's-degree level. Both were referred to as "mental health practitioners" by the Washington state Health Department. In the program, each counselor carried a case load of twelve to thirteen patients. We offered twenty-four-hour case management, including on-calls.

Five years later, I was transferred to the Health Care for the Homeless program. I was assigned to three homeless women's shelters to treat the mentally ill. My case load expanded to thirty to forty mentally ill women per week. While I was working in the mental health system, I also served Campus Ministry part-time. I founded the Church of Mary Magdalene for homeless women, and my case load grew to one hundred per week. Seven years later when the General Assembly put me on a speaking tour for six years, the whole country (several hundred churches) became my responsibility to motivate to end homelessness.

My confession is that God had disciplined and trained me systematically, raising my case load from a small number to huge crowds. God's plan to walk with me through this journey has been amazing! *I have no fear of dealing with these crowds. In fact, I love them.* In God's careful plan I became who I am today. Everything has been and will be in God's hands.

Therefore, "Amazing Grace" has become my song ever since.

I can conclude that God transformed all my toils and troubles into motivation to serve the Lord by serving the poor/homeless. It is my turn to share some of the abundant blessings I have received in this country with the poor and homeless around me. Thus, I have been serving the mentally ill homeless and substance addicted people for the past five decades as a mental health counselor/social worker/case manager and a Presbyterian minister up to this date (2018). It was my way of following my Jesus Dream. I will go on until my last breath because following the Jesus Dream is the core purpose of my life. Finally, "Here I am, Lord" in the Presbyterian Hymnal became my life-long song: "*Here I am, Lord. Is it I Lord? I have heard you calling in the night. I will go, Lord if you lead me. I will hold your people in my heart.*"

Appendix

Samples of Student Testimony

Testimony by **Karlene Vazquez**, a Criminal Justice Student at Northwest University (Given at the Second-Anniversary Celebration of Jean Kim Foundation)

Ladies and Gentlemen,

My name is Karlena Vazquez, a student of Northwest University. I am coming before you today to convey how the Jean Kim Foundation has impacted my life. I met Dr. Jean Kim, one Friday night at the homeless dinner of the Nest Mission in Edmonds. It changed my life forever. Dr. Kim had a booth set up with pamphlets explaining how she could help to enhance your education. I took  a pamphlet with me. It took a very long time to respond to the pamphlet.

One day I finally called Dr. Kim and asked her how she could help me. She told me that going back to college/university to further my career would lift me out of poverty, and lead me into a better-paying job and eventually to permanent housing. I explained how I had already received my associates of arts degree from the criminal justice program at Bellevue College in 2012, and I wanted to further my career as a legal advocate for battered victims, and that required my bachelor's degree. Dr. Kim went with me to the university to apply, she paid the application fee. Many nights Dr. Kim met me at the Lynnwood Library helping me apply for student financial aid.

She was always by my side through all of it. Because of her tireless help I got accepted at Northwest University. Dr. Kim paid for my first trimester's textbooks. Dr. Kim has taken me under her wing because she wants me to be successful. She has taken me out to dinners many times to make sure that I have nourishment. Dr. Kim has set up a tent city called Shepherd's

Village. It is temporary housing for homeless students. Dr. Kim invited me to live in Shepherd's Village. I lived there for three or four months, until I found permanent housing, August 1, 2017.

By encouragement, and support both financially and emotionally Dr. Kim has challenged and empowered me. She has also mentored me through all my struggles. She has promised to walk with me up to the podium to receive my bachelor's degree on my day of graduation. Thank you.

Testimony by **Mike Weyerts**, a Pharmacy Technology Student at Edmonds Community College (Given at the Second-Anniversary Celebration of Jean Kim Foundation)

I am Mike Weyerts, a student at Edmonds Community College studying to be a pharmacy technician. I am so happy to be in college. I am here this evening to say how Jean Kim Foundation changed my life:

I have come a long way in the past two to three years. I went through a divorce. My children live away from me. I lost my job as an LPN, became homeless, and have battled alcohol. I was very depressed.

Then I met Rev. Jean Kim at Nest Mission's Friday night dinner at Maplewood Presbyterian Church. Until the day I enrolled to EDCC last Spring quarter, she walked with me for the whole year meeting me several times a week encouraging, supporting as well as challenging and confronting me about my alcoholism and frequent relapse. I frustrated and disappointed her a lot. However, her persistent love and care about me compelled her to write a wonderful supporting letter to the court for my DUI charges. Her wholehearted pledge to work with me led the court to deter a year jail term to a year probation. I was so grateful. It was the grace of God.

While I was on probation she strongly encouraged me to pursue my college education further. So I followed through with my application for federal student aid by her recommendation. Before I knew it, I was already taking prerequisites, and now I am studying toward a certification as a pharmacy technician. She even helped me receive a bike and computer and paid for some school fees and ORCA cards and many other little items. I owe a huge thanks to God and the JK Foundation for changing my life. Thank you very much.

Testimony by **Tony Thompson** (Given at the Third-Anniversary Celebration of the Jean Kim Foundation, September 8, 2018)

I met Jean (Doctor/Reverend) Kim a few years ago. Seems like forever. I wandered into "neighbors in need" one Saturday looking for a friend. Whom I met and spoke to was Jean. Luther, I blame you… Heard her dream and being receptive to any call for help I later asked, "What did I just get myself into?" I remember thinking many times in the last couple of years.

Next thing I knew I had two students to tutor. Unfortunately, that didn't work out well, so she put me to work elsewhere. I had a few skills she discovered after getting to know me. Next thing I was working pretty much full-time. Helping with admin chores, computer work, editing. Heck…I even had to get her car jump-started a few times.

Next up came her idea of a secure camp for homeless students. NOW you are talking…right up my alley of expertise. I can design, estimate, and build this thing, yup. Meeting with Rev. Chris Boyer,who is the almighty at Good Shepherd Baptist Church, we had an idea. I did some research on borders, property lines and drew up a plan. We had actually garnered a little interest from the media and we all did a few interviews, lately a few more. Thanks to *The Everett Herald* and KIRO. Maybe a little leverage to the city of Lynnwood for our much-needed permissions and changes, its been a slow climb there. In steps Christine Frizzell. She has tirelessly continued her support, hard work, and drive to make this a total success. Many have collaborated in this project but the drive behind this has been Jean. She has and still is relentless. To all who know her she is a force to be reckoned with and almost impossible to say no to. I only know this all too well.

After building and seeing many who entered Shepherds Village I seem to have turned into a social worker…with no formal training. As an engineer this is not my training or patience level. Thanks, Jean (said sarcastically). You have taught me so much in the short time I have known you. I can say that many have been an influence in my life, but you have been a huge commanding force. Your drive and perseverance have made me a better person, so for this I thank you, my friend.

A few short months ago you called me and said your back was broken, YIKES! I gladly helped you get to a few of your doctor appointments, errands, etc. Not sure your trip to California to finish your autobiography and translation was a total success. Must have taken a bad step off the plane. Enter into assisted living and your move from your condominium, I know was a challenge. From 200 m.ph. to 10 was no small feat for you. I know you have been at lightspeed in your pursuit of your dream. I agree, and have been trying to help but rarely have I been able to keep up with you. How does that work out with our age gap?

Your retirement from the JKF has not been easy, for you or all concerned. Mr. Jason Dunbar has been the perfect choice to take the reins. Change it is never easy, but change is part of our world. Not easy, not bad but it is what it is. His organizational efforts are exceptional. An asset to this endeavor of yours. Your dream, Jean, will live on, I will make sure of that because I believe in you and your dream. That's what I signed up for and I want to see succeed. I have your back on this one. Take that to the bank . . .

Now talking about the bank, I have donated my time and a few funds. Its up to all of you to donate . . . maybe I should say dedicate some of your time, effort and money to Jean's dream. All who know me will understand I am not comfortable with asking, but I am asking now. Keep JKF and Jean's dream alive and I dare say mine too. Write a check, give some time, and help us out for this most worthy cause. To each and every student, keep your own dream alive to succeed in your continuing education and to eradicate homelessness. If we can help, we will. Just ask.

Samples of Sermons by Jean Kim

January 26, 2018
Sermon at Friday Worship Service of the Nest Mission
To my homeless friends
Scripture text: Luke 4:18-19
Theme: "We have a dream."

We Have a Dream

I want to continue with Pastor Luther's wonderful sermon last week celebrating Dr. King's birthday and his legacy and reflect on our own socio-economic-political crisis today. I will continue with his theme "I have a dream." I once was an activist for human rights and the peace and justice movement. I read many books in that regard. In my home library, I had four books written by Dr. King or edited by his wife, Coretta. I re-read them all to prepare this sermon. This evening, I chose Luke 4:18-19, which is Jesus's dream statement. Our sermon theme this evening is "**We have a dream.**" There is nearly no one who has had no dream. Our dreaming starts very early on when our parents ask us as a four- to five-year-old child, "What do you want to be when you grow up?" Then we used to answer, "I want to be a president, doctor, teacher, carpenter, or garbage collector, etc." Do you remember what your answer was?

My first point is what was Jesus's dream in his own time and context?
Luke 4:18-19 is a passage that is very well known to all Christians. I have been calling it "Jesus's mission statement." This evening I call it "Jesus's dream statement." Let's read it together. Let me try to paraphrase it: *The Spirit of the Lord is upon me, because he has anointed me to dream good news for the poor. He has sent me to dream release to captives, dream to restore sight to the blind, dream to let the oppressed go free, and dream to proclaim Jubilee.*

The Palestine world where Jesus lived was occupied and dominated by Romans. The whole country and people were oppressed and exploited every possible way politically, economically, religiously, and culturally. People were mostly poor peasants. The Jewish political/religious leaders played a puppet role to Roman power in exploiting their own people.

Peasants ended up paying high taxes to the Roman government as well as the Jewish nation. When they couldn't pay mounting taxes they had to get a loan, putting their land up as collateral and became debtors. They ended up losing their land when they couldn't pay their debts. Peasants became homeless and were turned into day laborers and slaves, and women into prostitutes. Uproars, suppression, persecution, mass crucifixion were quite popular practices.

In such a dark economic and political context, what was Jesus's dream?
Jesus uses the words "good news" for Dr. King's word "dream." Therefore, Jesus's good news is his dream. But in fact, he is saying "I have a dream." I have a dream that someday the poor will end their poverty. I have a dream that someday all captives in prison will be freed. I have a dream that someday all the blind will see a bright future. I have a dream that someday all oppressed will come out and dance for joy. I have a dream that someday the land robbed for debts will return to its owner. I have a dream that someday all slaves will be freed to unite with their families. I have a dream that someday all their debts will be paid off. I have a dream that someday a loud liberty bell will ring throughout Palestine. I have a dream that someday there will be no debts, no cross, no death. I have a dream that someday all Jews will sing the Jubilee songs.

How did he carry out his dream?
Jesus chose non-violent methods by only loving all people perfectly: The very foundation of Jesus's new kingdom rests on unconditional *agape* love. *Agape* loves the unlovable, even enemies. Jesus was the incarnation of God's love.

All powers hated his challenge to the oppressive system with love for the poor.

They killed him. Even on his death bed, the cross, he practiced non-violent love.

As John Shelby Spong describes, *when his disciples forsook him, he loved his forsakers. When his disciples denied and betrayed him, he loved the denier and betrayer. When his enemies abused him, he loved his abusers. When they killed him, he loved his killers. He gave his life away even as they took it from him. Here was a whole human being who lived fully and loved wastefully. He was thus the meaning of God, the source of life and love.* I would call him the very essence of the human dream.

His dreams appeared to be crushed before they were actualized. For the past 2,000 years, they continued to grow through others like you and me. We experience a much better world now, but we still have a long way to go.

My second point is what is Dr. King's dream?
He describes the life of black people as follows although it changed a lot over the years: *Being a Negro in America means being a part of the company of the bruised, the battered, the scarred, and the defeated. It means trying to hold to physical life amid psychological death. It means the pain of watching your children grow up with clouds of inferiority in their mental skies. It means having your legs cut off, and then being condemned for being a cripple. It means seeing your mother and father spiritually murdered by the slings and arrows of daily exploitation, and then being hated for being an orphan. It means the ache and anguish of living in so many situations where hopes unborn have died.*" In such a socio-political, cultural, economic context Dr. King announced his dream:

I have a dream that one day this nation will rise and live out the true meaning of its creed: "that all men are created equal." I have a dream that one day on the red hills of Georgia sons of former slaves and the sons of former slaveowners will be able to sit down together at the table of brotherhood. I have a dream that one day even the state of Mississippi, a desert state boiling with the heat of injustice and oppression, will be transformed into an oasis of freedom and justice. I have a dream that my four little children will one day live in a nation where they will not be judged by the color of their skin but by the content of their character.

Dr. King tried to achieve his dream through non-violent means by saying,
Hate is too great a burden to bear. Throw us in jail and we will still love you. Bomb our homes and threaten our children and, we will still love you.

We shall match your capacity to inflict suffering by our capacity to endure suffering. We will meet your physical force with soul force. Do to us what you will, and we will still love you. We'll wear you down by our capacity to suffer and one day we will win our freedom. We will not only win freedom for ourselves, we will win you in the process, and our victory will be a double victory. This will be the day when all of God's children will be able to sing with new meaning "My country 'tis of thee, sweet land of liberty, of thee I sing.

Such a non-violent approach reminds me of Jesus's way.

My third and last point is our dream in our own context
I have been serving the most underprivileged people in American context for nearly half a century. Most of you receive food stamps at $194 (2017) value per month, and can't even survive on it. Some live in low-income housing, but many **of you** couch surf or live in **your** cars. **Many of you** are financially, physically, emotionally, mentally, legally challenged with substance issues with rental and employment barriers. **Many of you** carry tons of tickets and debts. **Many of you** work, and yet don't earn enough to afford housing and living. In one of the largest continents of the world **many of you** cannot find a 6x6 space to pitch a tent. Amid millions of luxurious mansion homes, **you** don't have 8x8 tiny houses. **Many of you** are not healthy enough to do heavy labor work and many are not sick enough to be eligible for a **government** disability benefit. In the world's leading affluent country, you live like refugees in a war zone of third-world country. In a country where people sing peace and democracy and praise God with song, you live like throwaways. Many affluent people sing "God bless America." But you seem to know no blessings. Many moms and dads and children love and enjoy each other but many of your hearts are broken for having your families torn apart and your children taken away. When many sing the American Dream you sing a song of despair. Your dreams and hopes are being crushed and shattered. So I name homelessness "despair unto death" because many die young. Your future seems to be closed in on you as a dead-end with no job, no home, no hope. Many of you can join in this experience of crushed dreams.

What has been our reaction to our crushed dreams?
Many young people get angry and run into shooting spree. Many of my homeless friends are angry, resentful and hurt others and themselves by poisoning their mind and body with substances which is another form of violence.

Dr. King suggests that *such a reaction poisons the soul and scars our personalities.* He added that, "*Violence as a way of achieving justice is both impractical and immoral. It is impractical because it descends in destruction for all. It is immoral because it seeks to humiliate the opponent rather than win his understanding; violence is immoral because it thrives on hatred rather than love. It destroys community and makes brotherhood/sisterhood impossible.*

Violence ends by defeating itself. It creates bitterness in the survivors and brutality in the destroyers."

Dear friends, can we <u>still</u> have our dreams?

Can we dream Jesus's dream? Can we dream Dr. King's dream? Can we dream that one day everyone will have a job with a living wage? Can we dream that one day whatever hours one worked we can afford housing? Can we dream that one day there will be neither poor nor homeless? Can we dream that one day all of the tickets are canceled? Can we dream that one day our debts to housing and colleges are canceled? How can we dream such a dream amid all these crushing evil forces?

According to Dr. King, the answer *lies in our willing acceptance of unwanted and unfortunate circumstances even as we still cling to a radiant hope. You must honestly confront your shattered dream. Place your failure at the forefront of your mind and stare daringly at it. Ask yourself, "how may I transform this liability into an asset?"*

Many of the world's most influential personalities have exchanged their thorns for crowns. Dr. King gives some examples: Charles Darwin suffered from a recurrent physical illness; Robert Louis Stevenson was plagued with tuberculosis; and Helen Keller, inflicted with blindness and deafness, responded not with bitterness or fatalism, but rather by the exercise of a dynamic will, transformed negative circumstances into positive assets. George Frideric Handel's health and his fortune had reached the lowest ebb. His right side had become paralyzed, and his money was all gone. His creditors seized him and threatened him with imprisonment. For brief time he was tempted to give up the fight—but then he rebounded again to compose the greatest of his inspirations, the grand "Messiah."

My first dream was interrupted and shattered by the Korean War after one year of attending the best private junior high in Korea. It took **eight** months to get back to school in our exile. My honorable study abroad experience at the University of Chicago was shattered a year later due to financial hardship. It took **seventeen** years **for me to come back and** to finish my master's in social work at St. Louis University in St. Louis, Missouri. It took **twenty-eight** years for me to be ordained (by the Northwest Coast Presbytery, Washington) from the day of graduating from the theological seminary in Korea, due to many interruptions with life's struggles in the aftermath of Korean War. If you keep the torch of a dream burning, someday you get there to achieve your dream. We don't need to be chained to our life's troubles, tragedies and illness forever, but can turn all of them into a motivation to do something good for ourselves, others, and society with help from God.

Yes, we all can have our dreams. Despite your many obstacles many of you are going to colleges to attain your dream. Some of you are in job training. Many of you are working. My dream is to help as many of you as possible get into colleges and find work and housing until my last ounce of energy is exhausted.

You are here every Friday evening to ensure your dreams. Be strengthened, gain a new energy, and new plan and new commitment. You are here not just to eat the dinner but to examine your lives and perform a tune up. We will walk with you throughout your difficult journey of achieving your dream.

I want you to engrave these words, *"I have a dream"* in your heart, soul, and in your brain, and carry it with you by saying it every day, *"I have a dream."*

Let us all shout twice, "I have a dream! I have a dream!" Amen.

Sermon at Madrona Presbyterian Church:
May 15, 2011
Scripture text: Ex. 3:7-10 Matt. 4: 23-24
Sermon theme: Is God Out to Lunch?

This sermon was delivered to motivate the Madrona Church to open her basement and make a shelter for homeless families with children.

Is God Out to Lunch?

Thank you for inviting me to worship God with you this morning.

I preached here several times in the past. I am grateful to come back again. It is so good to see you again. I am the pastor emeritus of the Church of Mary Magdalene, which is a congregation of homeless women in downtown Seattle. I founded and have served this church for many years. After I retired from this ministry, Women's Ministries and the Hunger Program of the General Assembly hired me to go on a speaking tour to educate the whole PC (U.S.A.) church on homeless issues and present program ideas. I helped many churches to give birth to a homeless mission. I have also seen several hundred homeless programs churches are engaged in.

In the last few years, I and my colleagues have been challenging the Korean immigrant community to share their blessings with the local homeless people. With their support we ended up creating Nest Mission. I also helped develop the homeless Network of Seattle Presbytery to encourage churches to engage in serving homeless people. We need a representation from your church.

I chose my sermon title "Is God Out to Lunch?" from the scripture text of Exodus and Matthew we just read for you. What I am going to speak about this morning might be the preaching to the choir because you are all very familiar with homeless issues.

Have any of you ever felt that God was out to lunch during your troubled times?

My first point is asking "Is God out to lunch?"

A woman was attacked and raped in the night while sleeping in the park. In the struggle to run away, she broke her ankle. There was no one to help her. She might have felt God was out to lunch. A fragile homeless woman was knocked down on the Third Avenue, in bright daylight and pushed into a car, taken somewhere, and was raped for a few days. No one was there to help her. She might have felt that God was out to lunch. An elderly woman was sleeping by a dumpster in the alley between Second and Third Avenues. She was run over by a garbage truck and lost both legs. She might have felt God was out to lunch. Another woman was sexually abused by her clergy father for many years, this left her emotionally messed up for the rest of her life. She might have felt God was out to lunch. A woman with several children slept in her car as her husband was laid off from his work, and a low-income apartment didn't come up for a long time, she might have felt God was out to lunch.

In your King County, the 2010 one-night count showed 8,937 were homeless, of whom 55 percent were families with children. Too many people sleep in cars or outdoors these days. They might have been feeling God was out to lunch.

Mary's Place, which is a day program of the Church of Mary Magdalene, sees many more homeless families with little children pouring in every day. But they can't afford to keep them in motel rooms until Section 8 comes up. In their homeless life with uncertainty, loss, and deprivation, children experience damage to their brain function, life skills, social skills, and learning. Homelessness for women and children is a life-threatening trauma just like fire and tornadoes. Homelessness for women often means robbery, assault, rape, and even murder. Therefore, I named homelessness the "disease unto death."

Some of you might say, we have made it in our struggles, why can't they make it? People who have many problems are still housed when they have financial resources or families. People who are messed up too deeply can't make it on their own. They need help.

My second point is that God is NOT out to lunch.
Exodus 3:7-10 witnesses that God observed, heard and knew the misery of the people of Israel in Egyptian bondage. And God came down to deliver them from the oppressive Egyptians. God was actively working. God was NOT out to lunch.

Matthew 4: 23-24 witnesses that God in Jesus was busy walking on the streets of Galilee, talking and eating with sinners, healing the sick, and saving the sin-sick souls. God was busy. God was NOT out to lunch. The first century Christians witnesses that God was NOT out to lunch. They sold lands or houses, put the proceeds in a common pot and shared with the poor. Therefore, there was not a needy person among them. God was actively working through them. God was NOT out to lunch. God suffers with those who suffer. God is hungry with those who are hungry. God is in pain with those who are hurting. God weeps with those who weep. God is working with us every minute healing our wounds. God is NOT out to lunch.

My third point is that God wants us to prove by our loving action that God is NOT out to lunch.

God always looks for human partners. In our Exodus text, God did not work alone in liberating Israel. Through and with Moses, God ended Israel's homelessness in Egypt. In our Matthew text, God in Jesus Christ was on Galilee's streets saving people. In our story of Acts, God responded to the needs of people through the first-century Church. You too are called as God's partners to rescue homeless mothers and children. Mary's Place is desperately looking for a church that can open a room for homeless families.

What would you say if Jesus asks you to sell all you have and give it to the poor just like the first-century Christians did? You might say, "Oh, Jesus, are you out of your mind? We are poor and have nothing to sell." What would you say, if Jesus asked you to invite the homeless into your homes as Matthew 25:35 states? Would you say, "Oh, my Lord, Jesus, you know we don't have any extra room. Or would you say, "We don't know them. We fear them. We can't have them in our house." What would you say, if Jesus asks you to open your church facility for homeless families? Is that a better and more doable option than selling your house or inviting the homeless into your home? Or would you say, "Oh, Lord, Jesus, we are hosting a meal program already. That's enough, Lord." What would you do if he cries out to you, "I am dying out here on the streets in homeless children?" Are you going to walk away as if you heard nothing? Or are you going to open your facility and invite him in? Or would you say, "Oh yes, we will open for Jesus but NOT for the homeless!!" Do you remember Jesus said, what you have done for the homeless means you did it for him? Opening or not opening your church is a matter of choosing to be a country club church or Christ's Church. It is a matter of choosing to be a missional church or self-serving church. It is a matter of finding the identity of your Church or losing Jesus altogether.

My fourth point is about the missional church.
Dr. John Buchannan, former moderator of Presbyterian Church (U.S.A.) writes, "Mission is why we are here, and the church exists for the world." He quotes Theologian Emil Brunner saying. *"The church exists by mission as fire exists by burning."* McNeal, the author of *the Present Future,* claims that the North American churches suffer from severe mission amnesia. They have forgotten why they exist. The church was never intended to exist for itself. The North American church has lost its identity because it has lost its mission. Trouble is, the church is sleeping on the job. The modern-day institutional church exists to be self-serving. Wilbur Shenk, former professor of mission at Fuller Seminary, wrote, "The true test of religion is whether the people of God practice justice and live righteousness. This is measured by the way that the socially powerless—widow, orphan, and alien (the homeless) are treated.

It has been that way all along while I have been serving homeless people. If God is pleased with what I was envisioning, God always went ahead of me guiding my way with resources, so that I couldn't have any excuse to back off. I couldn't do anything but follow God's lead. When I was too slow God would pick me up and carry me on his back. I had no choice but doing what God wants me to do. Just as God chose Moses as a partner to go to the Pharaoh to deliver the Israelites from Egyptian bondage, Jesus needs Madrona Church to be his partner to rescue homeless families from devastating homeless crisis. If you choose to become Jesus's partner, you prove that God is NOT out to lunch.

I bring you a mission idea: If your church decides to open the space for homeless families and children, Mary's Place, which is day program of the Church of Mary Magdalene, will become your partner. They will screen and send you homeless families and help recruit some volunteers. During the day, families will go to Mary's Place to work out their problems. We can ask the WHEEL Program to offer you consultation on how to set up and carry on. Seattle Presbytery's Homeless Network will help recruit ten other churches in this area to be your partners, who can help with volunteers, meals, and needed resources. This will be a volunteer-run mission program by ten to twelve churches together. It is doable and is being done at Lake Burien, Northminster Church in Seattle, and in many other cities.

I have an awesome testimony to share with you: I befriended Deacon Park of the Nashville Korean Presbyterian Church in Tennessee when I led a mission revival service there last month. Ever since, he and I have been exchanging greetings through e-mails. I wrote to him that I would be preaching here this morning and that I will bring you a program idea to help homeless families with children, because we are getting more and more homeless in Seattle. He wrote me back sharing his early experience: When he was young in Korea, his musician father died. His mother couldn't pay the rent. One day they were evicted, and she called all their relatives with no luck. As a young boy, he and his family spent the night outside. So he understands the family crisis with no home. He added, "I mailed you $3,000 check today, which you may use any way you see the need." I wept as I was reading his e-mail, knowing that God is not out to lunch and God is busy walking even ahead of us hearing the outcry of homeless families with children. I will suggest Korean Nest Mission to designate that money as seed money to provide a shower room, mats, room dividers, etc. when your church sets up a shelter for homeless families. (That money is being deposited in its account for you temporarily because I didn't want to hold it.) All checks that come to me I will turn over to the Nest Mission.

No one has decided to open a room for homeless families yet, but God has already started to work. God is walking way ahead of us by providing us with seed money. There is no coincidence with God. Mary Magdalene Church told me about the plight of the homeless families, I was asked to preach here this morning, and a check came from Nashville, all of these came together in a couple of weeks' time. There is no other way to interpret this except announcing it as "God's doing." Through you and me and Mr. Park, God seems to prove that God is in control. I don't know how you feel about this, but it is an awesome spiritual experience for me that God is busy and not out to lunch.

My concluding remark for you this morning is that we owe Jesus our lives. This is our turn to pay him back a little by becoming helping hands for Him, who is suffering with the homeless out on the streets. When a poor church like Madrona, which has little, shares with the needy, then we know that God walks with us and is NOT out to lunch.

God never wants to owe you anything. So God will pay you back fully for what you will do. Proverbs 19:17 says, "Whoever is kind to the poor lends to the Lord and will be repaid in full." In Luke 6:38, Jesus says, "give, and it will be given unto you. A good measure, pressed down, shaken together, running over, will be put into your lap; for the measure you give will be the measure you get back."

May God set this church on fire for mission and growth. May God bless you abundantly for what you are just about to do. Are you ready to sing? "Here we are, Lord, we have heard you calling in the night. Send us Lord, lead us Lord, to hold your homeless families in our hearts." Amen.

Note: After this service, the leaders of the church met and decided to renovate the church's basement and provide it as an emergency shelter for the homeless families with children. Praise the Lord! Ever since 2012, this renovated basement has been a home for homeless families.

About the Author

Jean Kim was born in North Korea in 1935 and took refuge in South Korea with her family at eleven years of age. Kim emigrated from Korea to the United States in 1970. For most of her career in the U.S., she has served the homeless. Kim has served on dozens of church and/or social service committees, including the Washington state Governor's Advisory Council on Homelessness. She is an organizer, preacher, lecturer, workshop leader, and writer on homelessness, domestic violence, women's leadership in the church, and clergy sexual misconduct.

Kim was ordained as a Minister of Word and Sacrament by the North Puget Sound Presbytery in1987 (now Northwest Coast Presbytery). She is a retired minister and former staff member of the Presbyterian Church (U.S.A.) for the issue of homelessness. The Presbyterian Church (U.S.A.) sent her out on a speaking tour for six years to raise consciousness and educate the whole church to be actively engaged in the mission of ending homelessness in the U.S. Kim is also a Washington state certified social worker and a certified mental health counselor.

She is a graduate of Han Shin Graduate School of Theology, Korea (bachelor of arts in divinity, 1959); Dan Kuk University, Korea (bachelor of arts in English literature, 1960); St. Louis University (master of social work, 1977); and San Francisco Theological Seminary (doctor of ministry, 2006).

Kim is a founder and co-founder of the following fourteen mission programs:

Founder: the Olive St. Social Club (a day center for the homeless), Cherry St. Social Club (a day center of the homeless), the Church of Mary Magdalene (for homeless women), the National Korean American Coalition for the Homeless, the National Presbyterian Network to End Homelessness, the Northwest Presbyterian Network to End Homelessness, the Seattle Presbytery Network to End Homelessness, the Olympia Presbytery Network to End Homelessness, the Nest Mission for the homeless, Regional Presbyterian Networks to End Homelessness (Washington state) and International Ministry at the University of Washington Campus Ministry, and the Jean Kim Foundation for the Homeless Education.

Co-founder: the Agape Church for the Homeless, New Haven, Connecticut, and the Korean Community Counseling Center, Seattle.

Kim has received twenty-four community service awards, including the Women of Faith award from the Presbyterian Church (U.S.A.), the Medal of Honor from the Korean government, and the Hero of the Homeless award from the Nightwatch in Seattle.

Other Works by Jean Kim

Jubilee Manual: Jean Kim's End Homelessness (2000 in English)
Video: *Jean Kim's End Homelessness* (2000 in English)
Video: *Jean Kim's End Homelessness* (2000 with Korean caption)
Plant the Cross: Reality and Root Causes of Homelessness (2008 in Korean)
Is Women's Leadership Acceptable as t Is Now? (co-authored, 2009 in Korean)
Is Women's Leadership Acceptable as it Is Now? (co-authored, 2012 in English)
Hope in the Color Purple (2017 in Korean)
Hope in the Color Purple (coming in 2019 in English)

These writings can be found on her website: www.jeankimhome.com

Made in the USA
San Bernardino, CA
15 January 2019